REAL
SUCCESS

REAL SUCCESS

Patrick Mather-Pike

DEDICATION

To Carol: without your love and support, I probably wouldn't have started. I love you!

ACKNOWLEDGEMENTS

There are so many people who have played a role in developing my thinking and attitude that I couldn't possibly mention them all. Needless to say, I'm extremely grateful to everyone. I especially want to thank my wife, Carol, for all her encouragement and the long hours she put in editing and correcting; the book is much, much better for it.

My thanks also to:

- Tamaryn Leigh Charlton for the owl illustration. "Mr. Owl" has become a much-loved part of the book.

- Richard Mather-Pike and Kirsten Warneke for assistance with the cover.

- Mike van Deventer, Brian Sullivan, and Kirsten Warneke for beta reading and suggestions for improvements. Thanks especially for all the encouragement.

- Everyone who agreed to my using their quotations. Thank you for taking the time to reply to my request for permission and for the encouragement you offered.

Contents

INTRODUCTION

For the past many years I've been reading, listening to, and watching positive material. My very first introduction to the idea of positive thinking came from listening to Earl Nightingale on the radio as a young boy. I can't remember what it was titled, but there was a broadcast of a short piece every afternoon. It resonated with me, and I tried to listen every day.

My next exposure came in the form of a book—*The Greatest Salesman* by Og Mandino. At the time I was working in a bank, and two or three times a week at lunch time I'd walk down to the local bookstore and buy a book. One day I found Og's little book and I couldn't stop reading it. I still have it. It's over 40 years old now, stained and scuffed but still treasured. Since then, various mentors have introduced me to some incredible people and also to life-changing material from some of the world's greatest minds. And I'm still learning every day!

This book is my attempt to share some of this. It's a bringing together of all the ideas and practices I've learned about that have positively changed my life. I've tried to put the information across as simply and practically as possible. If this is your first exposure to the wonderful, liberating concept of using your mind to help you create your dream life, you'll find this book especially valuable because it is so simply written. However, no matter what level of personal development you are at, these ideas and concepts from some of the world's most successful people are priceless!

Just reading the book will stretch your mind, expand your awareness, and give you the knowledge to start creating a better future. If, however, you work through the exercises at the end of each chapter (the book is intended to be a *manual* for successful living), the benefits will be multiplied many times over. Spend a week on each chapter, putting thought and effort into the exercises. If you have the courage and discipline to work through the exercises thoroughly, I believe the results will be truly life changing.

The book is divided into two parts:

- The first part deals with our thinking—our attitudes and paradigms. They are the key to unlocking the door to a successful life.

- The second part deals with success habits which, if you develop them, will greatly contribute to your success.

After every chapter you'll be encouraged to write out a sentence or two concerning the lesson learned. By compiling these into a single statement, you'll find that you have completed a mission statement for your life at the end of the first section. Similarly, after the second section you'll have created an action plan. If you are wondering why you need to read your statements aloud every day, have a quick look at the chapter on self-talk for clarification.

My sincere wish is that, by the time 36 weeks are past, your life will be better than you ever dreamed possible. And that will just be the start! As you continue to apply and practice what you have learned, you will grow from strength to strength.

The thinking patterns and success habits you will have cultivated will continue to enrich and benefit you for the rest of your life. You'll be more successful (according to your definition of success) and will reap a harvest bigger than your wildest dreams. In addition, you'll find that you will become a positive influence on those around you, enriching and stimulating them. The spinoff will be enormous if you are prepared to share what you have learned with others.

Picture each one of us as starting a ripple in a pond. Together we can make a positive difference in the lives of hundreds and thousands of others and leave a legacy for a better future.

Once you're finished with this book, make a point of reading the books in the recommended reading list. Invest in seminars, CDs, and DVDs. Make yours a life of continuous learning and growing.

So start today! God bless.

P.S. If you'd like a free, printable version of all the exercises and the tables for the time management chapter, go to www.realwealth.co.za/books and use the code you'll find at the end of the book to open it.

Part One

ATTITUDES AND PARADIGMS

Chapter 1

DEFINING SUCCESS 1

*"I believe that being successful means
having a balance of success stories across
the many areas of your life. You can't truly
be considered successful in your business
life if your home life is in shambles."*
—ZIG ZIGLAR

In today's world, many people think of success only in terms of financial success. If we drive a luxury car, live in a big house, and wear designer labels we're assumed to have made it. This, obviously, is a rather narrow view of success, which is why I like Zig's definition. It makes us think in broader terms about what exactly success is.

We are the only beings on the planet that have any notions of success or failure. It's part of what makes us human. Having a well-balanced view of success will give us the best chance of creating a successful life.

I remember reading a Tom Hopkins book years ago in which he tells of a man who lived under an overpass on the freeway. He had a mattress and blankets, was safe from the elements, got his food from a dumpster behind a nearby restaurant, and spent his days sitting in the sun swopping yarns with his friends—utterly content with his life.

Perhaps we should consider whether this man is more successful than someone else earning a six-figure monthly income in a high-powered job he hates. On one level, possibly; but on another level we can ask, what contribution is a man like this making?

Here, I think, lies the crux of defining success—are we successful if all we ever do is please ourselves? Or do we need to be making a positive difference in the world around us as well? I believe both—because we will never be fulfilled if we aren't making a difference and we will never be truly happy unless we are at peace with ourselves. True success is being well-rounded, making the best of every area of our lives.

So what should we be doing in order to ensure we create a successful life for ourselves?

First, I believe we need to realize and accept that it is up to us. No one can do it for us. We need to take time to define what success is for us. We need to decide what we want to achieve in each area of our lives.

Second, we need to craft plans as to how we are going to achieve what we want. The sad thing is, most people stumble though life never giving any time to thinking about how they would like their lives to be. Yes, they may sometimes wish for a better life, but they never really make time to actually think about it, never mind actively plan it.

So let's start today.

For this week consider the following:

Define what success is for you in the following areas:

- Health: Bear in mind that without your health, nothing else really matters.

_____

_____

_____

_____

_____

- Relationships: Remember that relationships are the basis for all success. Think in terms of family, colleagues, and friends.

_____

_____

_____

_____

_____

- Finances: What do you consider to be financial success?

_____

_____

_____

_____

_____

- Career: Considering that we spend approximately one third of our lives working, what will give you the most satisfaction?

_____

_____

_____

_____

_____

Take time this week to think about each of these areas of your life and to write a defining statement describing how you'd like each to be. Discuss each with your partner, if you have one, or with a trusted friend. Once you have decided exactly what it is you want, it'll be that much easier to start planning what you need to change in order to achieve it.

Now write out your definition of success as concisely as possible and read it aloud every day.

Chapter 2

DEFINING SUCCESS 2

"Success is 'The progressive realization
of a worthwhile dream or goal.'"
—EARL NIGHTINGALE

M any people think of success in terms of having arrived.
They see success as a destination.

The problem with this thinking is most vividly illustrated by the fact that many Olympic athletes suffer from depression after winning medals. I remember listening to one gold medalist telling how she burst into tears once she realized that everything she had lived for up to that moment was over. It took her months to come to terms with the fact that her whole life up to that point had been focused on just one thing— winning gold. Once she did, she had no other goal, no other motivation. In fact, she felt that there was no meaning to her life anymore.

Many great motivators teach us that it's not the succeeding that's important, but what we become in the process. Having goals, plans, and the determination to achieve them forces us to grow personally. As we overcome the challenges we all face on the way to succeeding, we become better people. Our self-belief, our self-confidence, and our self-image all improve, and that is worth more than anything.

Along the way we may inspire others, make some worthwhile contribution to our community, or even society in general. We may create some lasting legacy or some invention that benefits the human race. The possibilities are endless!

Too often we put life on hold until.... Bad idea! Brian Tracy calls it living in *"someday isle."* One day when we've graduated; when I get that promotion; when the kids are out of the house; when we retire; we'll do.... In the meantime, life passes and we miss all the good that's going on around us right now. Life is short and we should endeavor to enjoy every minute, because we don't know which will be our last. So, while having goals and striving to achieve them is critical for our success, we should always remember to stop and smell the roses along the way.

We need to keep in mind that success is a journey and that, in the process of striving to achieve our goals, we should enjoy the ride and value the lessons we learn along the way.

This week take some time to consider what kind of person you'd like to become in the process of working toward your goals—more self-confident, a better leader, a better parent, etc.

List these characteristics.

_____

_____

_____

_____

_____

_____

_____

_____

_____

_____

_____

In light of the above, review your definition of success and alter it if necessary.

Read aloud every day.

A final thought on this. If you're not moving forward in your life, not realizing your goals, why not spend this week deciding what it is you truly want and how you can achieve what you want. Experts tell us that the simple act of writing it down is the starting place of all success.

Chapter 3

ATTITUDE 1

*"Nothing can stop the man with the
right mental attitude from achieving his
goal; nothing on earth can help the man
with the wrong mental attitude."*
—THOMAS JEFFERSON

Attitude—the way we think—is something that affects
our entire lives. In fact, attitude determines how our
lives turn out.

That's a scary thought for many people to accept, but to
me it's the most exciting thing I've ever learned! "Why?" you
may ask. Because I realized that only I can control my thinking and, if it's true that how we think determines how our lives
turn out, then by controlling my thinking I control my life! I
think you'll have to agree that's exciting!

If you're reading this for the first time, you may be skepti-
cal. *"My thoughts determine my life's outcome? Who says so?"*

Well, first, the Bible: *"As he* [a person] *thinketh in his heart,
so is he"* (Proverbs 23:7).

Follow that up with just about every great philosopher in history—here are just two examples:

- Marcus Aurelius: *"Our life is what our thoughts make it."* He also said: *"The happiness of your life depends upon the quality of your thoughts."*

- Khalil Gibran: *"Your living is determined not so much by what life brings to you as by the attitude you bring to life; not so much by what happens to you as by the way your mind looks at what happens."*

Now consider that no one can make you think anything. Only you have the final say on what ideas, thoughts, or people you *allow* to influence your thinking. Perhaps now you can begin to understand how important controlling your thinking is. Our thoughts determine our feelings, our feelings determine our actions, our actions determine our habits, our habits determine our results, and our results determine our life's outcome. It all starts with how we think.

This is awesome—and sobering—because it also means that where we are in life right now is a result of our past thinking and not because of what someone else did or didn't do. We can no longer blame our parents, teachers, spouse, etc. for our present situation. It's our responsibility.

Those who have the courage to accept this as true will end up changing their lives to whatever they want them to be. The bottom line is to train ourselves to look for the positive in every situation, to expect everything to turn out for the best, and to consistently act accordingly. Not easy. In fact, Wallace D. Wattles, in his classic *The Science of Getting Rich*, said that it's the hardest labor in the world. This is why 99 percent of people in the world live in poverty and failure or, at best, mediocrity. They either don't know or they're not prepared to put in the mental effort. It also explains why 1 percent of the world's population controls 95 percent of all the money in the world. They do know, and they were prepared to put in the effort!

So, starting today, we need to become aware of exactly what it is we're thinking about most, because we gravitate toward our dominant thoughts. Simply put, if we're constantly thinking about lack, that's what we'll attract more of. If we're constantly thinking illness, unhappiness, failure, etc., we need to change and start thinking about what it is that we want (health, happiness, success, etc.). Thoughts are energy, and we need to stop giving energy to what we don't want and start giving energy to what we do want.

THOUGHTS = FEELINGS = ACTIONS = HABITS = RESULTS = LIFE'S OUTCOME

This week spend some time thinking about how you habitually think.

Are your thoughts predominately positive or negative?

_____

_____

_____

_____

_____

_____

Do you regularly put yourself down or build yourself up?

_____

_____

_____

_____

_____

_____

Are you argumentative or do you generally strive to be a peace-maker?

_____

_____

_____

_____

_____

Do you continually criticize or do you look for the best in everyone and every situation?

_____

_____

_____

_____

_____

Write a concise statement detailing your new attitude to life. Say something like *"I am always positive; I see only the good in everyone and every situation."*

_____

_____

_____

_____

_____

Read this aloud every day, along with your success definition.

Chapter 4

ATTITUDE 2

*"Whether you think you can, or you
think you can't—you're right."*
—HENRY FORD

To briefly recap, in the last chapter we learned that our attitude (the way we think) determines our life's outcome.
In other words, where we are right now in life is a result of
our past thinking. As I said, this is exciting, because it means
that we are responsible for our present circumstances—we
can't blame anyone else. It also means we are responsible for
our future!

Changing our attitude from negative (focusing on what we
don't want) to positive (focusing on what we do want) is the
single most important thing you can do to change your life.
Not only will it influence your success, it will also improve
your health, your relationships, your finances, and your spiritual life. I think you'll have to agree that it'll be worth making
the effort. In case you're doubtful about all these benefits,
do some research; there are studies proving everything I've
just said.

The exciting thing is that it takes just 30 days to create a habit or, in this case, change a habit—negative thinking. The first step is to become aware of what we are habitually thinking. Until we start consciously monitoring our thoughts, we won't be aware of how negatively we think. Unfortunately, the normal inputs we receive are mostly negative. From the moment we are born, we are constantly bombarded with negative messages: *"Don't do that," "You can't...," "Stop dreaming and be realistic,"* and so on. In addition, the media continually bombards us with negative news. Is it any wonder that we automatically develop a negative outlook?

Start becoming aware of each thought, and if it's negative, reject it and replace it with a positive thought. For example, if you find yourself thinking *"I can't...,"* reject it and say to yourself *"I can do this."* If you catch yourself thinking negative thoughts about someone, stop and actively focus on that person's good points (we all have at least one or two!). We can replace whatever negative thoughts we have with positive ones. After doing this for just 30 days, it will become habitual and you'll find your whole outlook will have changed for the better.

A fantastic way to reinforce this is to start telling ourselves good stuff—known as positive affirmations. Over 90 percent of all conversations we have, we have with ourselves. We are constantly talking to ourselves in our minds, and because of our negative conditioning, what we say is generally self-defeating and often self-destructive. Remember that what we focus on we attract, so only tell yourself what it is you want. For instance, if debt is a problem, don't talk about debt—not even getting out of debt, because debt is still the focus. Instead, talk about being financially free. Do this with emotion and as if it's already happened. *"I'm so happy and grateful that I am financially free!"*

At the same time, actively avoid all negative inputs. None of us is bullet proof, and if we allow negative in, it becomes that much harder to remain positive. Understand that negative grows unasked for (like weeds in the garden), so we have to actively eliminate it. The Bible urges us to *"guard your thoughts because they are the source of true life"* (Proverbs 4:23 CEV) and to *"take captive every thought"* (2 Corinthians 10:5 NIV). Good advice!

This week, make a list of all your inputs. In other words, what do you read, watch, and listen to?

List them below:

HELPFUL INPUTS	UNHELPFUL INPUTS

HELPFUL INPUTS	UNHELPFUL INPUTS

Now decide on a plan of action to increase the helpful inputs and decrease the negative ones.

_____

_____

_____

_____

_____

_____

Write a concise statement of what you are going to do. For example, say something like, *"I only watch positive, uplifting programs on TV."*

_____

_____

_____

_____

_____

Add it to your previous statements and read aloud every day.

Chapter 5

DREAM BIG DREAMS

"Dream lofty dreams, and as you dream,
so you shall become. Your vision is the
promise of what you shall one day be."
—JAMES ALLEN

The ability to dream, to see the future before it is, is one of the characteristics of humans. No other species, to our knowledge, has this ability. Dreams are the starting place for every great invention, undertaking, journey, building, relationship, career, etc. In fact, dreams are essential for the progress of the human race. Without someone dreaming, no progress is possible. Why? Because everything starts as a thought—a dream!

Dreams are critical to our success. Without a vision of the future, there is no motivation to act, no incentive to try, no reason to grow. Children dream instinctively; you just have to watch them at play to see this. They create fictional people, places, and events in their imaginations that keep them entertained for hours.

Unfortunately, society soon discourages us from dreaming and there is pressure to conform. Teachers and parents tell us to stop dreaming and be realistic. Sadly, most of us do, diminishing the most powerful faculty we humans have— imagination. As Walt Disney said, *"Every child is born blessed with a vivid imagination. But just as a muscle grows flabby with disuse, so the bright imagination of a child pales in later years if he ceases to exercise it."* Without imagination (dreams) we might as well be dead. Life has no excitement, no anticipation, without dreams to look forward to.

Spend time this week dreaming of your perfect lifestyle. Imagine your perfect relationships, career, home, vacations. Do not for one moment stop to consider whether it's possible; just decide how you would like your life to be. Imagine that you cannot fail and that money is no object.

Have fun describing, in detail, your dream home, car, career, vacations, family relationships, etc.

_____

_____

_____

What would you start doing?

_____

_____

_____

_____

_____

What would you stop doing?

_____

_____

_____

_____

_____

Now summarize all the above into a single, concise statement.

_____

_____

_____

_____

_____

Add it to your previous ones and read aloud every day.

Chapter 6

THINK BIG

*"There is no passion to be found playing
small—in settling for a life that is less
than the one you are capable of living."*
—NELSON MANDELA

Think big! It's something we hear regularly from all the success gurus. It's almost become a cliché. However, these two words are probably two of the most important words we will ever hear. As we are learning, our dreams and our attitude are the keys that unlock our future. Small dreams unlock a small future, so it's vital that we develop big dreams.

Thinking big is the starting place of all great success, simply because how we think determines how our lives turn out. We become what we think about most. Unfortunately, most of society seems to conspire to limit our thinking and keep us from ever achieving our full potential. Often it's those closest to us who are the worst culprits. *Don't get your hopes up. Be realistic. What makes you think you can do that?* These are the kind of comments we most often hear from family and friends.

It isn't that they consciously want to hold us back; it's just that they unconsciously don't want us to leave them behind. Having the courage to ignore these comments is the mark of achievers.

Next come our own self-doubts and limitations. Most often we are our own worst enemies, putting ourselves down in our minds before we even attempt anything new. What we need to start doing is to concentrate on what we have already achieved and build on that rather than concentrating on our perceived failures. Note, I said *perceived* failures, because that's exactly what they are. You see, we all operate out of our own perceptions, and what we perceive as failure someone else will perceive as a stepping stone, a valuable lesson to be learned on the road to success.

How we think is crucial to our success. We will achieve exactly what we think, whether we think big or think small. As Andrew Matthews says in his book *Being Happy*, "*Perhaps one of the most important principles you will ever understand about your mind is that you will always gravitate toward what you think about most.*" The key is to constantly be thinking big, expecting the best—not the worst. Each one of us was endowed at birth with more talents and abilities than we could ever use in our entire lifetimes. Thinking big is the catalyst to discovering just how much we can do. The exciting thing is that the more we achieve, the more we come to believe that we can do more, and more, and even more!

So start today to think big about everything. Start thinking about how you think. Are your thoughts predominately big, or are they small? Do you habitually expect things to turn out right, or do you expect to fail? Every time you find yourself thinking small thoughts, stop and consciously think about how you can turn whatever you're thinking around into bigger, better, best! By doing so, you will begin to change your life into the one you've always dreamed of.

This week make a note of every time you think small thoughts.

List them below and then rephrase them to be big thoughts.

SMALL THOUGHTS	BIG THOUGHTS

Now identify your most frequent small thought (the one that holds you back the most) and write a statement expressing it in a positive way, a big way. For example, if you find you're constantly thinking *"I can't do...,"* rephrase it to say *"I'm fantastic at...."*

_____

_____

_____

_____

_____

_____

_____

_____

_____

_____

_____

Add to the previous week's statements and read aloud every day.

Once you've turned this "small thought" into a strength, go back to your list and pick the next most frequent one and repeat the process.

Chapter 7

BELIEF

*"It's what you choose to believe that
makes you the person you are."*
—KAREN MARIE MONING

What we believe is critical to our success in every area of our lives.

Recently, my wife and I were listening to a CD and were so encouraged by what one of the speakers said. I want to share this because it occurred to me that belief is one of the most important attitudes we can develop.

On the CD, the Reverend Michael Beckwith relates the story of how some years ago his ministry was in a situation of having to move premises. The lease on their current building was up and the new building needed renovations before they could move in. With time and money running out the congregation were despondent. Reverend Beckwith called a meeting of his governing committee and, once they were all in the room, locked the door. *"No one leaves until we all agree that it's possible for us to move on time."* Various objections were voiced—no money, lack of time—but he countered all of them by saying that what he was asking was not *how* or *when*, only if it was *possible*. Finally, everyone agreed "*Yes, it was possible.*" Reverend Beckwith goes on to tell how, within a week of the meeting, the money became available, the contractor called to say he would work overtime at no extra cost, and the building was completed on time—such is the power of *belief.*

So many times in our lives, when faced with challenges we look at the circumstances and, based on what we see, we give up on our dreams and goals. Doing this is a guarantee of failure. Believing that it is possible, on the other hand, opens our minds (specifically our subconscious mind) to coming up with solutions and actions that will enable us to achieve what we want. As Terry Pratchett wrote in *Hogfather*, "*You need to believe in things that aren't true. How else can they become?*"

Belief is a habit, and it must be nurtured and strengthened by constant exercise. Belief can also be called faith, and the Bible has some interesting things to say about faith. Jesus said that if you have faith like a mustard seed you can move mountains (see Matthew 17:20). Too many of us see the words *mustard seed* and miss the real point. You either have faith or you don't; there are no degrees of faith. It's like being pregnant—you either are or you aren't. You can't be slightly pregnant!

So we either believe it's possible and act accordingly, or we don't. The exciting thing is that it's a choice and only we can make it. Believing and acting accordingly will activate the Law of Attraction (also known as the Law of Sowing and Reaping), and we'll begin to draw into our lives what we need to succeed.

This week, spend some time thinking about your basic beliefs. Think in terms of money, success, relationships, responsibility, and self-image. Write them down—say something like, *"I believe money is...."*

▪ Money

_____

_____

_____

_____

_____

▪ Success

_____

_____

_____

_____

_____

- Relationships

_____

_____

_____

_____

- Responsibility

_____

_____

_____

_____

- Self-image

_____

_____

_____

_____

Now think about whether your basic beliefs are helping you move forward or holding you back. Think about rewording the beliefs that are holding you back to change them into positive beliefs that will help you move forward.

Write a concise statement for each one.

_____

_____

_____

_____

_____

_____

_____

_____

_____

_____

Choose the one that you feel is your biggest challenge and add it to the previous weeks' statements and read aloud every day.

Once you're satisfied that you've overcome this, take the next biggest challenge and repeat the exercise until you've turned all the challenges into strong, positive beliefs.

Chapter 8

Self-Image

> *"Believe in yourself! Have faith in*
> *your abilities! Without a humble but*
> *reasonable confidence in your own powers*
> *you cannot be successful or happy."*
> —Norman Vincent Peale

Our self-image, how we think about ourselves, is the most important factor in our success as human beings. Quite a statement, you might say, but I honestly believe it to be true. Our self-image will determine our expectations, our relationships, our happiness, our self-confidence, our finances, and our ultimate success.

The amazing thing is that researchers tell us that 95 percent of five-year-old children have a great self-image, yet by the time we get to 18 years old, only a small percentage still do.

What went wrong? Basically, we listened to people around us saying, *"You can't do that, you'll fall, be careful, don't get your hopes up, be realistic,"* etc. We stopped dreaming and started *settling*—a guaranteed self-image destroyer.

The most important thing in life we can do for ourselves is to continuously build up our self-image. Here are a number of simple yet highly effective things we can do:

1. Understand that each of us is an awesome creation, absolutely unique. There is no one else with our fingerprints, our precise blend of talents and abilities, our mindset, and our thoughts. Surely God wouldn't have gone to all the trouble of creating someone so unique just for them to be a failure. *You* are awesome!

2. Realize that the only opinion that counts, in the final analysis, is our own. Terri Cole Whitaker wrote a great book entitled, *What You Think of Me Is None of My Business*. People's opinions are just that—opinions. They are based on their perceptions, their hang-ups, and are *not* fact. So never let other people's opinions negatively influence you.

3. Realize that what other people say is not nearly as important as what we say to ourselves. Over 90 percent of our conversations are with ourselves, and if we're constantly putting ourselves down, we've got a problem. Start focusing on all the things that are good about you. Tell yourself daily (in fact, many times a day) why you can, why you deserve to succeed, etc. Say, *"I like myself, I'm special, I'm a winner, I can do it."*

4. Become goal orientated. Setting goals, no matter how small to start with, and working toward achieving them is a fantastic way of boosting our self-image. Every time we achieve a goal it reinforces that we are capable, that we can succeed, and our self-belief increases. Setting and achieving goals is a fantastic self-motivator and stimulates us to keep aiming higher. The more we achieve, the more we believe. The more we believe, the more we try, and it becomes a positive upward spiral of success.

5. Understand that no one is perfect; that failure is an event, not a life sentence; and that the most successful people in life are also the ones who have failed the most. In fact, quit using the word *failure* altogether (it's very negative), and start thinking in terms of temporary setbacks. It's only by experiencing setbacks that we learn and grow stronger.

Focus on the big picture and not on the setbacks and detours life hands us. I love what Jack Canfield says: *"Life's just lifing; it's not personal."* If we keep our focus on our dreams and goals, we won't get sidetracked by life's little mishaps. As the saying goes: *"When the dream's big enough, the facts don't count."* So don't let setbacks affect your self-belief and self-image—you are special!

This week take time to list the things that make you special. Think in terms of:

- Things you're good at

_____

_____

_____

_____

_____

- Past successes

_____

_____

_____

_____

_____

_____

- The times your skills have helped others

_____

_____

_____

_____

_____

- The times your ideas have solved problems

_____

_____

_____

_____

_____

Now summarize all the above into a single, concise statement. Say, "*I am special because....*"

_____

_____

_____

_____

_____

_____

_____

_____

_____

_____

_____

_____

_____

_____

Add it to your previous ones and read aloud every day.

Chapter 9

WHO AM I?

"This above all—to thine own self be true.
And it must follow, as the night the day,
Thou canst not then be false to any man."
—WILLIAM SHAKESPEARE

Who am I? It's a question we've been asking ourselves ever since creation. Most philosophers, poets, and thinkers have probably spent some time pondering the answers. As Deepak Chopra said, *"Who am I? It's the only question worth asking and the only one never answered."* That, I think, is a pretty normal response to the question—most people seem to be unsure of the answer.

However, I don't believe that the question has never been answered; it has been, clearly and distinctly. The Bible tells us exactly who we are. We are made in the image of the Creator, we've been gifted with talents and abilities beyond our understanding, and we are sons and daughters of a king (the King of kings).

So let's take a look at just exactly who we are. The starting place is to realize that we are unique creations. There is no one else quite like us on the planet. No one has our fingerprints, our thoughts, our potential. As Nasir Siddiki explains, *"You were born a winner—there were approximately 250 million sperm racing to get to the egg first and you made it."* You started winning at conception, so don't stop now!

When you were born you had a mind far superior to any computer yet made. You were capable of learning at a rate that still astounds us, and more importantly you were capable of reasoning, something no computer can do. You have more potential than you can ever use. In fact, psychologists tell us that we only ever use about 10 percent of our brain power. Can you imagine what we could do if we really tried?

The only limitations we have are those we place on ourselves and physical ones. I, for instance, am a small person. I could never have played rugby for the Springboks! Physical limits aside, there's nothing you and I can't do. As Napoleon Hill said, *"Whatever the mind of man can conceive and believe, it can achieve."* You need to realize that you already have everything you need to succeed in any field you choose.

Now I know this sounds crazy, but think about it this way. Our history books teach us that Guglielmo Marconi invented the radio, the Wright brothers engineered flight, Thomas Edison created the light bulb, Marie Curie developed x-rays, and so on.

But, did they really invent these things *or* did they merely figure out how to utilize what was already there? Radio waves, electricity, the laws governing aeronautics, and x-rays have all been in existence from creation, someone just figured out how to use them. Everything mankind needed to progress and succeed has been in place since the beginning. It's the same with you; whatever you need to succeed you already have—you just need to figure out how to use it. Jesus taught that if you have faith (in other words, if you believe), nothing will be impossible for you (see Matthew 17:20). Living a successful life, then, ought to be a piece of cake!

Our problem isn't not knowing who we are; rather, it's not knowing who we aren't. We are not too stupid, too slow, too tall, too short, or whatever label we put on ourselves. We are uniquely gifted wonders of creation, capable of anything we put our minds to. We have been gifted with *all* the talents and abilities we need to succeed, in whatever field we desire. All we have to do is believe in ourselves and never stop trying. Anyone who's ever watched the Special Olympics should be convinced that nothing is impossible for the person who really wants it.

So start today to look at yourself as you really are—a wondrous, unique creation with more potential than you can ever use. Never let anyone tell you otherwise. You are a winner! No matter what has happened in the past, you can change and you can succeed. I'll leave you with one of my favorite quotes (by George Eliot): *"It's never too late to be what you might have been."*

Write down all your good points—the things that make you special.

_____

_____

_____

_____

_____

_____

_____

_____

_____

_____

_____

_____

_____

Go back to last week's statement about why you are special and alter it if necessary.

Add it to your others and read aloud every day.

Chapter 10

WHY AM I HERE?

*"You are not here merely to make a living.
You are here in order to enable the world
to live more amply, with greater vision,
with a finer spirit of hope and achievement.
You are here to enrich the world, and you
impoverish yourself if you forget the errand."*
—AUTHOR UNKNOWN

Here's another question that every one of us has asked at some time in our lives: "Why am I here?" Or, as it is often posed, "What's the meaning of life?" It's one of those fundamental questions that philosophers and thinkers have been pondering for centuries.

Plato said we are here to attain the highest form of knowledge, in his view: *"Good, from which all good and just things derive utility and value."* Aristotle added that we need to go one step further. Not only do we need to study good, but we need to become good as well.

Every religion has its version of an answer. The Buddhists believe we are here to strive for enlightenment (Nirvana);

59

Islam says we are here to worship Allah; Christians believe that our purpose is to glorify God and preach the Good News of salvation throughout the world.

Whatever our backgrounds, I believe we were put here to make a positive difference. My favorite explanation comes from Eugene Peterson's *The Message*: "*Let me tell you why you are here. You're here to be salt-seasoning that brings out the God-flavors of this earth. ...You're here to be light, bringing out the God-colors in the world*" (Matthew 5:13-14 MSG).

In order to make a difference, I believe we have to become the difference. We have to set the example in our actions and our words. There's a saying that "*you can't give out what you haven't got.*" So for us to make the greatest possible difference, we need to become all that we are capable of becoming. Personal development and people skills are the key. The more we grow as human beings, the more we learn to relate to those around us and the greater our impact on the world can be.

It all starts with our thinking, our *attitude*. As we've noted in previous chapters on attitude, everything starts with thought. What we think ultimately becomes our reality. So the starting place for growth and success is to understand exactly how we think about things. For instance, what do you think about money? Is it something you never have enough of, something only meant for others (the greedy rich), the root of all evil? Or is it something you're worthy of having in abundance, a tool to make your life comfortable and to help others? However you think will determine how much you have.

The next step is to strive to become a more successful person in every aspect of our lives. The more we grow and develop, the more we are able to help others. The exciting thing is that striving to become all that we are capable of becoming is a lifelong pursuit. It's a journey that has no end. It gives meaning and purpose to our lives, keeping life interesting and exciting.

Striving to become more encompasses every area of our lives—physical, mental, spiritual, social, and economic. When we embark on a lifelong quest to become better, we find that our lives become so much more satisfying, so much more meaningful. We'll come to like ourselves more (the prerequisite for liking others), become better spouses, better parents, better employers or employees—in short, a positive influence on those around us. We'll be healthier, happier, wiser, and richer.

So starting today, make a commitment to yourself, and then to those nearest to you, to start working on yourself. Invest in yourself by reading positive books, listening to positive CDs, and watching positive DVDs. Avoid negativity at all costs, because what you put in comes out. Get around people who will challenge you and stretch your thinking. Start looking for ways to make a difference in society. In the process, you will find your life becoming more satisfying and meaningful.

Write down ways in which you can be of service to those around you.

_____

_____

_____

_____

_____

_____

Summarize it into a concise statement of intent. Say something like, *"I make a positive difference in my community because...."*

_____

_____

_____

_____

_____

_____

Add it to your others and read aloud every day.

Chapter 11

GRATITUDE

*"The more you express gratitude for
what you have, the more you will
have to express gratitude for."*
—ZIG ZIGLAR

Having an Attitude of Gratitude will make all the difference
to our happiness and success.

Most people go through life focusing on what they don't
want and don't have, thereby attracting more of the same into
their lives. Developing an attitude of gratitude changes our
focus to what we do want and do have, attracting more good
into our lives. It's one of the most rewarding habits we can
develop because we increase not only those things that we
want, but also our appreciation of life in general. We become
happier, healthier and wealthier! A profoundly good deal, I'm
sure you'll agree!

So how do we go about developing an Attitude of Gratitude? The starting place is to make a habit of counting your
blessings every day.

Just the simple fact that you woke up this morning is wonderful—about 156,000 people didn't! The fact that you are reading this means you are literate (about 560 million aren't), you have a roof over your head (about 100 million don't), and you had money to buy this book (about 842 million people don't have enough to eat!).

Are you feeling better yet?

Now consider the following: Do you have two eyes that work? How about two hands, two feet, two ears, two kidneys? There are many who don't.

How much value would you attach to them? Put another way, would you be prepared to sell an eye, a hand, or a foot for a million dollars? I think not! Health truly is our greatest wealth, and we live in a time when people are living longer than ever before and, if we take good care of ourselves, are healthier than ever before. Advances in medical science have rid the world of so many of the scourges that killed our ancestors—cholera, polio, smallpox, etc. Today, chronic diseases are rampant, but excitingly, with simple lifestyle changes, we can do a lot to prevent them.

We are all so blessed in so many ways. We live in countries where we are free to read what we want, say what we want, travel where we want, own property, and earn a living. We have access to shelter (homes), water and electricity, medical care, retirement benefits, shops full of food and clothing, and much more. We have families who love us and friends who care about us.

Best of all, we have the ability to dream and to turn those dreams into reality. Today it has never been easier to turn a good idea into money. In fact, there are many who have become incredibly wealthy doing just that. Think of Bill Gates, Steve Jobs, Elon Musk, and Mark Shuttleworth, to name just a few. With just one good idea, a positive attitude, and lots of dedication and hard work, each of these men has become fabulously wealthy. What's stopping you?

Never before have we had access to so much information about success, personal development, creating wealth, etc. We are surrounded by amazing people who will inspire us, whether in person, on CDs and DVDs, in books, or on television. There is an abundance of information available to help us create happy, healthy, and wealthy lives for ourselves. All we have to do is make the effort and the time to put it to use.

On top of all this, there is a God in heaven, the Creator of all the universe, who loves you! He tells us that He knows how many hairs are on our heads, that He's set His angels to watch over us, and that He works everything for the good of those who love Him. Truly something to be grateful for!

Make it habit to start and end every day by consciously thinking of all the things you can be grateful for. I learned a wonderful way to do this from Bob Proctor, who suggests we say, *"I'm so happy and grateful that...."*

This week take time to make a list of everything you have to be grateful for.

_____

_____

_____

_____

_____

_____

Now summarize all of the above into a single concise statement. Start it with, *"I'm so happy and grateful that...."*

_____

_____

_____

_____

_____

_____

Add it to your other statements and read aloud every day. Keep changing it as your life progresses and you have more and more to be grateful for.

Chapter 12

EXCELLENCE

*"The quality of a man's life is in direct
proportion to his commitment to excellence,
regardless of his chosen field of endeavor."*
—VINCE LOMBARDI JR.

Around 400 BC Aristotle said: *"We are what we repeatedly
do. Excellence, then, is not an act but a habit."* There are
two important lessons we can learn from this quotation to
help us develop an attitude of excellence.

First, *"we are what we repeatedly do."* We have learned
that our lives are shaped by our thoughts. Our thoughts determine our feelings, which determine our actions. Our actions
become our habits, and our habits determine our results.
It all starts with how we think. Developing an attitude of
excellence, therefore, is the starting place for developing an
excellent life.

The second lesson we can learn from Aristotle is that
results require effort. *"Excellence, then, is not an act but
a habit."* Developing an attitude of excellence requires

consistent effort before it becomes a habit, which, in turn, will give us the excellent results we are looking for. This effort will be well worth it!

The starting place is a decision. Make a decision to do the very best you can in all you do. Decide to do more than you're paid for, more than is expected.

Look at your list of dreams from Chapter 5, then decide how you can become better in every area relating to those dreams. For example, if you want promotion, decide to become the best employee in your company. Start today to learn everything possible about your job and how it affects the rest of the company. Find out how you can improve what you do so that it will positively impact everyone in the company associated with you. Come early and stay late. Be the one willing to help others, even though it isn't part of your job description. Your boss will soon notice, as will other department heads, and you'll be the one picked for promotion next time around.

If you want better relationships with family and friends, decide how you would like others to treat you and then take the initiative and start treating them that way. Soon you'll notice a change in the way they treat you, and your relationships will become joyful and satisfying.

Changing the way we are and what we do changes the way the world reacts to us. Being excellent in all that we do causes the world to react with excellence in return, attracting the good we desire into our lives.

Do not, however, make the mistake of trying to achieve perfection. Perfection is not possible for us mortals, and striving to be perfect will just lead to discouragement and add stress to your life. Rather, aim to be the best you can be in every situation.

At this point I need to stress that it won't happen overnight; it takes time. The good news is that the benefits will be exponential. The compound effects will astonish and delight you, but you need to be patient and persevere. Don't expect overnight changes or instant results. Remember the story of the tortoise and the hare. Become a little bit better each day and your future will take care of itself.

Make a list of all the areas of your life you want to improve.

_____

_____

_____

_____

_____

_____

Now decide what you need to do in order to become excellent in each of the areas you've listed.

_____

_____

_____

_____

_____

Summarize the above into a concise statement.

_____

_____

_____

_____

_____

Add it to your previous ones and read aloud every day.

Chapter 13

RESPONSIBILITY

"Accept responsibility for your life.
Know that it is you who will get you
where you want to go, no one else."
—LES BROWN

In this chapter let's look at another aspect of success—responsibility.

By this I mean accepting personal responsibility for our actions. It's not a popular idea these days—most people would rather talk about their rights, conveniently forgetting that with rights come responsibilities. They are Siamese twins—one cannot survive without the other.

The beauty of accepting personal responsibility for our actions is this: if we don't like our results (what's happening in our lives), all we have to do is change our actions. No one else is involved. We don't need to get approval or permission from anyone, because we accept that what happens to us (our results) is simply the result of the actions we take and we have sole choice in deciding our actions.

I think it was Steven Covey who first pointed out that responsibility is actually made up of two words—*response* and *ability*. Of all God's creatures, we are the only species that has the ability to choose our response to things that happen to us. Animals react—it's either fight or flight. Most humans also react this way. However, we are unique in that we have a third alternative—we can think about the situation and decide on the best course of action.

Today it's fashionable to excuse poor results/bad behavior by blaming someone else—our parents, teachers, the government, society, whoever! However, when we do that we give away our power to control our own lives. By refusing to accept that we alone make the final choice in how we act, we put ourselves in subjection to the one we blame for our situation. We become a slave to someone else. Admittedly we're not physically enslaved, but we are very definitely mentally enslaved.

As I have already said, by accepting full responsibility for our actions we take control of our results, because our actions determine our results. Taking this one step further, when we take control of our results we automatically take control of our futures!

To me this is one of the most exciting concepts I have ever learned. It means that I am in control of my life and no one can influence the outcome without my permission! Yes, there are people who have input, but I get to choose who they are and to what extent they input into my life. It's totally liberating!

It's not easy to change bad habits, but it is possible. Psychologists tell us it takes 30 days to develop a habit, so obviously it will also take 30 days to break a bad habit.

We can't actually break a habit—we have to replace it with another habit. So from today, stop blaming others or circumstances for what's happening in your life. Accept that you and you alone are responsible for your actions. You choose your course of action. In 30 days you'll have changed the habit and will be on the way to creating a wonderful, successful life.

Response + Ability
It's my call.

This week take time to note how you view your current situation in life. Are you blaming others or circumstances for where you are right now? Write down those things you feel have led to your current situation and what choices you made in each instance.

_____

_____

_____

_____

_____

_____

_____

Now decide that from now on you are going to accept absolute responsibility for your actions and decisions. Write out a concise statement describing your decision. For example: *"I choose my actions and take responsibility for them."*

_____

_____

_____

_____

_____

Add this to your previous ones and read aloud every day.

Chapter 14

ASSOCIATION

*"You are the average of the five people
you spend the most time with."*
—JIM ROHN

Who we associate with, in person or by influence, plays a huge role in our success. Association simply means who we allow to input into our lives. The exciting thing is we can, to a large extent, control this. As we've learned in previous chapters, we become what we think about most. So who we listen to the most is very important, whether we actually speak to them, read what they have written, listen to CDs, or watch DVDs.

Charlie "Tremendous" Jones said: *"You are the same today as you'll be in five years except for two things, the books you read and the people you meet."* He lived his life teaching people the importance of association. He made a big impact in our lives and in the lives of tens of thousands of people all over the world. His book *Life Is Tremendous* is worth investing in.

We need to be very choosey about who we allow to input into our lives, because that input will affect our thinking and, ultimately, our whole life!

So let's have a look at each of the above mentioned inputs—people, books, and CDs and DVDs.

People are the most important because they often have the power to influence us the most. Epictetus said: *"The key is to keep company only with people who uplift you, whose presence calls forth your best."* If we want to succeed in life and achieve our dreams, it's important that we associate with people who will encourage us and believe in us. So stay away from the negative people out there who will pull you down, ridicule you, and try to steal your dreams. The sad truth is that they will often be the people nearest to you—family and friends. Understand that people without ambitions and dreams will feel threatened when you decide to do something special with your life and will try to talk you out of it. Then there are people who misguidedly want to protect you from getting hurt, not realizing that if you never try, you never succeed. It's often these people who are the most difficult to avoid.

Look at who you are associating with the most. Are these relationships building you up, having a positive influence on your future, or are they negative, sapping your joy and ability to lead a successful life? We become like the people with whom we associate, as illustrated by a study from Harvard Medical School. They tracked over 12,000 people for 32 years and found that those with friends who had become obese had a 57 percent greater likelihood of becoming obese themselves. So make it a habit to get around like-minded people who'll help you reach your dreams and goals.

Next are the books we read. Reading is an exceptionally important tool for success. There's a saying that *"leaders are readers,"* and studies of scores of successful men and women bear this out. The world's greatest people are willing to share their success secrets with you. All you have to do is read what they have to say. So make it a habit to associate with them by reading biographies, self-improvement, and motivational books. A really powerful success tip is to read something positive every night before going to sleep. Just 15 minutes of positive reading will give your subconscious mind plenty to work on while you're asleep, and you'll be amazed at the results.

Investing in and listening to or watching good CDs and DVDs will also make a huge difference to your success. One of the greatest things I ever learned was to use my car as a university. All the hours we spend in cars today can become an incredible asset if we make it a habit to switch off the radio and all the negative news on it and listen to positive CDs instead. Invest in CDs and DVDs that will motivate, inspire, and educate you.

Our mind is the greatest tool we have to help us succeed. We need to guard what we put into it as if our life depended on it—because it does! So make sure that whatever you watch on TV is positive; avoid watching programs that are violent and negative. Similarly, pay attention to the music you listen to—are the lyrics positive? Start today to be very careful about who you associate with—in person, in a book, or via your TV, radio, or mp3 player.

This week make a note, each day, of who you associated with and what you read, watched, and listened to. Was each a positive or a negative influence?

_____

_____

_____

_____

_____

Now make a list of the people you want to associate with who will inspire and uplift you. Decide what book you'll start reading, what CD you'll listen to, what DVD you'll watch. At the same time, decide who and what you'll avoid because they are/it is a negative influence.

_____

_____

_____

_____

_____

_____

Lastly, write a concise statement of intent detailing what you have decided to do. Say something like, *"I only allow positive to enter my mind, so I only associate with _____, read _____, listen to _____."*

_____

_____

_____

_____

Add this to your previous statements and read aloud every day.

Chapter 15

CHOICES

*"It is our choices, Harry, that show what
we truly are, far more than our abilities."*
—J.K. ROWLING

We came into the world without choice. We couldn't choose our parents, nor our time or place of birth. From then on, though, just about everything that has happened to us has been a result of the choices we made!

This may sound startling, but think about it. The choices we make every day determine how our lives turn out. These choices are the result of how we think, and only we have control over our thinking. No one has the power to force us to do, think, or say anything without our choosing to do so. The sad thing is that most people never stop to consider how they think. Their thinking is inherited from someone else—parents, teachers, friends, the media, etc. So their choices, and consequently their lives, are not always the best for them.

I hope that this chapter will get you thinking about the choices you make every day. Choices like being happy

(Abraham Lincoln said: *"Most people are about as happy as they make up their minds to be."*), being healthy, being successful, living a life that's meaningful, making a difference, and leaving a legacy.

The biggest challenge we have is not that we intentionally make bad choices. Rather, it's that we don't consciously make good choices. Have you ever been bitten by a whale? What about a mosquito? The point is that it's the little things in life, repeated over and over again, that will make all the difference. As Darren Hardy, editor of *Success* magazine, said, *"We sleepwalk through life"* not aware of the choices we are making and, as a result, never living our lives to the full. The compound effect of lots of little choices, ones we don't think about, can have a profound effect on our lives, good or bad. The key is to consciously start making choices that will enhance our lives. It's only by thinking about the future and actively defining how we want it to be that we can begin to make the correct choices to ensure it becomes our reality.

Let's look at some areas that will have a huge impact on our futures. For me, the first area must be spiritual, because I believe that life on earth is just the beginning. I once heard of someone telling an atheist that he didn't have the faith that the atheist had. The atheist was dumbfounded, as he had no faith, and asked for an explanation. The believer replied: *"Well I believe in life after death, heaven and hell, so if I'm wrong there's no problem. But what if you're wrong?"* I'd rather not take that chance; how about you?

Next is health. Today the world's population is being destroyed by chronic diseases—heart disease, cancer, diabetes, and mental degeneration like Alzheimer's. The amazing thing is that every health authority in the world tells us that these diseases are a result of lifestyle choices. They are the result of years of bad eating, lack of exercise, and other personal choices like smoking, drinking, and substance abuse. The choices we make today will most definitely determine our health status in years to come. Please don't think "*it won't happen to me*"—it will, unless you actively choose to maintain a healthy lifestyle now, especially if you're young.

Then we need to consider all the other areas of life—relationships, career, wealth creation, social contribution, etc. The wonderful thing is that we can choose to create a magical, fulfilling life for ourselves simply by making the right choices every day. The alternative is not making conscious choices, sleepwalking though life, and living a life of mediocrity and, at the worst, complete failure. The choice is yours.

As author Brodi Ashton said, "*Heroes are made by the paths they choose, not the powers they are graced with.*"

We make our choices then our choices make us!

Make a list of the things most important to you in your life.

_____

_____

Now list the choices you are making daily. Do they make those important things better, worse, or unchanged?

Write a concise statement of what you now choose to do to improve each of the important things from today forward.

Add this to your others and read aloud every day.

Chapter 16

WISDOM

*"There is more profit in it than there
is in silver; it is worth more to you
than gold. Wisdom offers you long
life, as well as wealth and honor."*
—**PROVERBS 3:14,16 GNT**

Some time back I read an article by Alexander Green on wisdom and it occurred to me that it really is a key to success. Yes, we can work on having a *positive mental attitude* and develop all the *success habits*, but you know what? Without wisdom we probably won't make the effort or have the ability to benefit from doing so.

My dictionary defines wisdom as the possession of experience and knowledge, together with the power of applying them critically or practically. I think you'll agree that this is a profound definition. We've often heard that *"knowledge is power,"* but without the wisdom to use it wisely, what's the point?

Just where and how do we acquire wisdom? I think the key is contained in the definition—*possession of experience and knowledge and the power to apply them.* We need to start by developing the habit of *continuous learning* (see Chapter 30) by reading books, listening to CDs, and attending as many seminars as we can. In short, getting as much information as we can about the things that will make our lives better. This includes a wide variety of topics ranging from finance to relationship skills to spiritual growth.

Today we are blessed with more information than ever before in the history of the human race. We have an almost inexhaustible treasure chest of data from books, CDs, DVDs, and the Internet. Never before have there been so many seminars and audio and video conferences available to us. Never before have there been so many success coaches, mentors, and gurus out there wanting to share their knowledge with us. Every month new books on success are being published. No one has an excuse for ignorance any more. If we don't know, it simply means we've been too lazy to make the effort to find out.

However, as we've already noted, knowledge is only one part of wisdom. In addition to knowledge we need experience, because it's experience more than any other single thing that allows us to use the knowledge *"critically or practically."*

We have all been taught at some time in our lives that *"experience is the best teacher."* That's not the whole truth. Other people's experience is the best teacher. Someone, somewhere, has been there before us and can save us an enormous amount of time, frustration, and effort if we're willing to learn from them. Because we don't have the luxury of enough time to experience everything, we should learn from those who have gone before us, if we're clever.

I think that, in addition to knowledge and experience, wisdom encompasses a few more characteristics. Things like integrity, kindness, tolerance, patience, generosity, and humility spring to mind. The ultimate goal of wisdom should be to live a happy, meaningful life, making a positive difference in the world and leaving all those we come into contact with better off than before they met us. It's doing and being as well as knowing.

So start today to do all you can to increase your wisdom. Read good books, listen to CDs, watch DVDs, attend seminars, and find yourself a good mentor. Don't simply accept what is spewed out by the media, politicians, and those around you. Learn to question everything you hear and make up your own mind.

If we become wise, I believe that when Judgement Day comes we'll hear those long hoped for words *"Well done, thou good and faithful servant"* (Matthew 25:21). In the meantime, we'll be better able to craft a happy, successful life for ourselves here on earth.

I'll end with a line from Alexander Green's article: *"Wisdom is an elusive concept. It entails a combination of knowledge, experience, discretion and maturity, a sense of what is best worth knowing and doing."*

Make a list of all the things you are going to do to increase your wisdom. Think in terms of books to read, courses to attend, people you'd like to get around (from whom you can learn), etc.

_____

_____

_____

_____

_____

Write a concise statement describing what you intend to do.

_____

_____

_____

_____

_____

Add this to your others and read aloud every day.

Chapter 17

INTEGRITY 1

"Integrity is not a conditional word. It doesn't blow in the wind or change with the weather. It is your inner image of yourself, and if you look in there and see a man who won't cheat, then you know he never will."
—JOHN D. MACDONALD

Perhaps the most important of all values, and possibly the hardest to sustain, is integrity. It's a word seldom used today when describing what the world calls success, yet without it I don't believe there is any true success.

Integrity, defined in the Oxford dictionary as *"wholeness, entirety, soundness, uprightness, honesty,"* is more about character than skill. You either have it or you don't; there are no degrees of integrity. It's like being pregnant—you either are or you aren't. I believe that having integrity means always doing and saying what is right, true, and fair. It's having a set of values that govern your life and living your life by them no matter what. It means not cutting corners, not saying one thing and doing another, not pandering to public opinion, not taking the easy way out. As Oprah Winfrey said, *"Real integrity is doing the right thing, knowing that nobody's going to know whether you did it or not."*

So many of the problems facing society today can be traced to a lack of integrity. Great leaders who inspired us with their integrity, like Mahatma Gandhi and Nelson Mandela, are few and far between. Worldwide in politics, business, sport, on TV, and in films we see examples of the lack of integrity that will, I believe, be the ultimate downfall of our civilization unless we change.

The exciting thing is that you and I *can* do something about changing this. By living our lives with integrity; by teaching our children to do the same; and by setting the example for our families, friends, co-workers, and employees we can show others the right way to live.

Many people complain endlessly about the problems, yet continue to add to them by their example. Every time we go through a red light, fail to stop at a stop sign, give bad service, do sloppy work, illegally dump trash or rubble, cheat on our taxes, etc., we are setting an example—a bad one. People are always looking at us, whether we are a parent, an employer or a superior, and what we do influences them. We can ensure that when people look at us, they see a good example. Just as the random acts of kindness movement spread and flourished worldwide, let's start a movement that sets the right example every time and encourage others to join.

Warren Buffett made a very interesting remark about integrity. He said: *"Somebody once said that in looking for people to hire, you look for three qualities: integrity, intelligence, and energy. And if you don't have the first, the other two will kill you. You think about it, it's true. If you hire somebody without [integrity], you really want them to be dumb and lazy."* In other words, if they don't have integrity they *will* cause harm. John Stuart Mill said: *"Bad men need nothing more to compass their ends, than that good men should look on and do nothing."*

Let's make integrity non-negotiable in our lives, teach it to our children, and demand it of our leaders.

Write down how you rate yourself as a person of integrity. Consider things like telling lies, breaking laws when you see you can get away with doing so, doing personal stuff in the boss's time, etc.

_____

_____

_____

_____

_____

_____

Now write down what you plan to change to make integrity a core value in your life.

_____

_____

_____

_____

_____

_____

Write a concise statement describing yourself as a person of integrity.

_____

_____

_____

_____

_____

_____

Add this to your previous ones and read aloud every day.

Chapter 18

INTEGRITY 2

"If humanity does not opt for integrity we are through completely. It is absolutely touch and go. Each one of us could make the difference."
—R. BUCKMINSTER FULLER

Integrity seems to be a word that has almost ceased to have meaning from a personal perspective. Now I know that this sounds extreme, but bear with me. I did an Internet search of the word. On the first ten pages there was not a single entry relating to an individual or a story about an individual. They were all listings for either organizations policing the integrity of various professions, organizations or industries or advertising companies or products with the word in their title. Surely integrity must be hopelessly lacking when there are so many out there checking on it (or more likely the lack of it) or trying to use it to sell their company or product (by implying that they have it).

Integrity, to my way of thinking, starts at an individual level and then percolates upward through every level of society. It's impossible for it to work any other way. Governments can't legislate it into existence, nor can organizations enforce it, because it needs to be a core value of individuals. Today many governments have fallen into the trap of thinking that by simply passing a law they can change behavior. It's never going to happen. The only way to change behavior is to set an example that the populace will want to follow.

All this may seem negative, but not so—because we *don't* have to wait for governments or policing organizations. We can start with ourselves right now, right where we are! We can start setting the example in our families, in our work places, in our businesses.

So what exactly am I suggesting we do? I think we should define for ourselves the core values we want to build our lives on (and our children's lives, seeing as we set the example for them). Values like honesty, reliability, excellence, punctuality, service, generosity, fairness, and tolerance.

Let's take a closer look at these values.

Honesty

For me, this means always doing what is right, irrespective of what's easy, popular, or what peer pressure demands. Don't steal, cheat, or lie.

Reliability

Always being true to our word. If we say we're going to do something, others can take it as done. So many people seem to have no pride in their word. Businesses promise the earth and don't deliver, people make appointments with no intention of keeping them, etc. Wouldn't it be wonderful if every time someone promised something we could be certain that it would happen?

Excellence

Having pride in doing the very best we can do in every situation. Review the chapter on excellence for more thoughts on this.

Punctuality

When we are late we waste other people's time. This is inconsiderate and rude.

Service

The Bible says we were put here to make a difference—by serving. A true leader is one who serves others by showing them the way. This means we have to set a good example wherever we are.

Generosity

This is so much more than being free with money. We can be generous with our time, with our praise, and with our patience, as well as with our money.

Fairness

Is what we think, do, and say always fair to all concerned?

Tolerance

Do we allow others to have their own views, or do we try to force ours on them? Are we patient with people who are different from us?

So let's *all* start doing what we can, and by our example set in motion the change we want to see in our society.

Go back to last week's exercises and re-look at them in the light of what we've discussed above. Revise if necessary.

Chapter 19

FAILURE 1

*"When I was growing up, my dad would
encourage my brother and I to fail. We would
be sitting at the dinner table and he would
ask, 'So what did you guys fail at this week?'
If we didn't have something to contribute, he
would be disappointed. When I did fail at
something, he'd high-five me. What I didn't
realize at the time was that he was completely
reframing my definition of failure at a
young age. To me, failure means not trying;
failure isn't the outcome. If I have to look
at myself in the mirror and say, 'I didn't try
that because I was scared,' that is failure."*
—SARA BLAKELY

For most of us, failure is something to be avoided at all costs.
For many successful people, failure is just a natural con-
sequence of always striving to improve. The above quotation
absolutely blew my mind the first time I read it. How I wish I'd
had someone to encourage me like that when I was growing

up. My next thought was how I wish every parent in the world could read it!

If we look at kids, they have no notion of failure. They just naturally push the boundaries all the time. That's how they learn. A baby starts trying to walk, falls flat, gets up, and tries again. A youngster tries to rollerblade, falls flat, gets up, and tries again. Later on they try to ride a bike, swim, climb onto the roof, make a bomb, whatever. They're always trying something new, and in the process they find out how not to do things.

I wonder when do we suddenly stop trying, and why? Is it because our parents or teachers kept telling us not to try in case we got hurt? Or is it peer pressure to conform to the norms of the particular culture we're associated with? Whatever the reason, it's a terrible thing to do—to stop trying.

The bottom line is that unless we keep trying to improve, whether it's learning new skills or trying out new things, life is going to rapidly pass us by. What we need to understand is that failure is not a life sentence, it's an event. Just because we failed to achieve something or got hurt in a relationship, that doesn't mean we can never win again. Too many people go into survival mode after a failure, build a wall around themselves, and never venture beyond it. As a result, they miss out on so much in life. Life is very short and time passes so fast. When we understand that time is not hours, minutes, and seconds (that's just how we measure time) but the measure of our lives, we'll be less inclined to waste it by not making the most of opportunities.

There is absolutely no disgrace in not achieving what we set out to do, as long as we learn the lessons and grow because of the experience. Think about every great invention or achievement of mankind. Didn't it involve a lot of trying and a lot of failing? Every great love story includes the risk that it might not work. The disgrace comes in giving up, in not getting up and trying again. In today's fast changing world, we have to keep growing if we want to keep up. Whether it's financially, technically, or relationally, we need to be constantly growing in order to make the most of all the fantastic opportunities available to us.

Never before in the history of the human race have we had so many opportunities to excel. The Internet, for instance, has made it possible for anyone, regardless of education, background, financial status, whatever, to have their own business and make a success of it. As long as we keep trying we can succeed, often beyond our wildest dreams. Yes, there will be setbacks along the way—that's life. The key is to keep trying and never give up.

This week list all the "failures" you've had in the past.

_____

_____

_____

_____

_____

Now list all the lessons and benefits (the *silver linings*) that resulted from them.

_____

_____

_____

_____

_____

Write a concise statement of why you are grateful for and better off because of the lessons and benefits you got. For example: *"I'm grateful that everything I do helps me to grow and learn."*

_____

_____

_____

_____

_____

Add it to your others and read aloud every day.

Chapter 20

FAILURE 2

*"Some failure in life is inevitable. It
is impossible to live without failing at
something, unless you live so cautiously
that you might as well not have lived at all.
In which case, you've failed by default."*
—J.K. ROWLING

In the previous chapter, we looked at the failures we've experienced so far in our lives and listed all the good that has come as a result of them. In hindsight, we often find that there is far more good in failure than all the perceived negative. That's because it's mostly our perceptions that make the failure negative. It's only when we start to see failures as stepping stones and not as stumbling blocks that we'll be able to overcome our fear of failing.

Not only is failure an essential ingredient to our becoming successful, but also to our continuing to be successful. Recently I watched a short video by Robin Sharma entitled *Nothing Fails Like Success.* It's a pretty weird title, don't you think? It's also very effective, because it gets one's attention immediately. He makes the point that often success leads to individuals and companies becoming complacent, arrogant, and/or lazy. When this happens, learning stops and soon the success starts to disappear. He quotes the example of a company that at one time was one of the world's leading cellular phone companies. They eventually lost major market share to opposition companies. Why? Simply because the founders became complacent and started coasting instead of continuing to innovate.

The very thing that made them successful in the beginning—innovation—caused their decline as the other companies "out-innovated" them and took away their superiority in the market place.

What's all this got to do with failure? Well, often we become complacent and stop doing the basic things that brought us success. Maybe we started treating others with contempt or impatience. Maybe we stopped the little daily disciplines that made us successful, or maybe we simply got lazy. For whatever reason, we started to fail.

Whether it's in our careers, our businesses, or our relationships, failure is more often the result of what we stop doing than what we are doing. When we get to the stage in any situation that we stop striving to improve, things are sure to take a turn for the worse.

The lesson we need to learn is that failure is often a good thing, simply because it serves as a wake-up call. It's a message that we need to review our actions and get back to the basics that made us successful in the first place. If we're lucky (alert enough), we get the message before there's too much harm done. If not, things go backward fast and become that much harder to fix. I like what George Bernard Shaw said: *"I dread success. To have succeeded is to have finished one's business on earth, like the male spider, who is killed by the female the moment he has succeeded in courtship. I like a state of continual becoming, with a goal in front and not behind."*

Take time to review the essential actions that made you successful in every area of your life, be it career, sports, or relationships. If things are not going according to plan, try to identify times when things started slipping and the lessons you learned or should have learned.

Write down the times in your life when things started going backward.

_____

_____

_____

_____

_____

Now take a good, hard look at what you did to get back on track and the benefits that resulted from the lessons learned.

_____

_____

_____

_____

_____

Go back to last week's exercises and revise your statement, if necessary, to include what you've learned this week.

Chapter 21

EXCUSES

"The person who really wants to do something finds a way; the other person finds an excuse."
—AUTHOR UNKNOWN

One of the biggest causes of under-achievement is the habit of making excuses.

Making excuses is our way of shifting the responsibility and/or the blame somewhere other than ourselves. As long as we do this, we give the excuse power over us and our future. Making excuses robs us of our chances of achieving anything significant in life.

More importantly, every time we make an excuse we reinforce our subconscious belief that we are not capable of achieving. This leads to loss of self-esteem and self-confidence—two of the most important attributes we need in order to lead a successful, fulfilling life. Because the problem with habits is that we do them without thinking, the first step in breaking the excuse habit is to become aware of every time we do make an excuse. We need to mentally catch ourselves and begin to hesitate before making the excuse. One way to do this is to repeat the following mantra over and over to yourself every day: *"Excuses are useless! They rob me of my success, my self-confidence, and my self-esteem. I take action and make things happen!"* Repeating this (or something similar that resonates with you) to yourself many times a day will cause your subconscious mind to alert you to the fact that you are making an excuse. This will help you to check yourself and start recognizing the excuse. Get someone close to you, whose judgement you value, to help you by gently pointing out when you make an excuse. Once you're aware, it becomes easier to stop.

The second step is to recognize that excuses are just rationalized lies. I'm certain that no one wants to be thought of as a liar, so start to accept that every time you make an excuse someone will think you're lying. Now that may not be the case every time, but think of it as actually happening. Next time you make an excuse to someone, immediately think to yourself, *"They think I'm lying."* It's embarrassing, especially if you're making the excuse to someone whose opinion you value. Remember, too, that your own opinion of you is the most important opinion of all. If you can't look yourself in the eye in the mirror and be proud of the person you see, life has little chance of being satisfying.

The third step in stopping the excuse habit is to actively start thinking of the benefits you'll receive by doing what you are currently avoiding doing. Before you make the excuse, now that you are aware of it, take a few minutes to think about all the good things that could happen if you did whatever it is. It could be an improvement in your relationships, a feeling of satisfaction and accomplishment for doing a task, an increase in earnings, whatever. The point is, there is always a benefit derived from taking action. Even if it is only learning what doesn't work, it'll save you making the same mistake or wasting the time in the future.

Make a list of the excuses you commonly make.

_____

_____

_____

_____

_____

Now list the things you're being robbed of by making these excuses.

_____

_____

_____

_____

_____

List the benefits you'll experience because you no longer make excuses.

_____

_____

_____

_____

_____

Write a short sentence stating how decisive you are and how taking action drives you to success. For example: *"I constantly take action and make things happen."*

_____

_____

_____

_____

Add it to your others and read aloud every day.

Chapter 22

FORGIVENESS

"The truth is, unless you let go, unless you forgive yourself, unless you forgive the situation, unless you realize that the situation is over, you cannot move forward."
—STEVE MARABOLI

The past is gone forever; it's history. Good or bad, we cannot change a thing that happened. All we have is now, and what we do now will affect our future. Unfortunately, some people never let go of the past. They either think in terms of *"the good ole days,"* missing all the good that's happening around them presently, or they go through life blaming people or events in the past for their present situation. Holding grudges and unforgiveness traps one in the past and prevents happiness and progress in the present. This, in turn, affects our future.

Often, someone goes through life bitter about some event or comment that is long past. The sad thing is, 99 percent of the time they are the only ones affected by whatever they're bitter about. Generally speaking, the person they are uptight with doesn't have a clue of their feelings. They carry on life totally unaffected by the negative feelings of the grieved party.

If this describes you, *decide* to let it go. Forgive whoever has hurt you. If they are aware of your negative feelings toward them, don't delay in going to them and saying, *"Let's put this behind us."* Not only will you be set free to move ahead, but so will they, so the reward is doubled.

The other aspect of unforgiveness is not forgiving yourself for past mistakes. Again, it results in a diminishing of the present and the future. When it comes to forgiving yourself, it's good to remember that whatever happened was done with the knowledge and experience that you had at that time. Some time back, I heard of a fascinating survey of top executives. When asked, "With hindsight, what percentage of decisions turned out to be wrong in the course of time," the answer was an astounding 70 percent! Now if Fortune 500 companies' top executives (who are trained, and paid, to make decisions) only get it right 30 percent of the time, how on earth can we get upset about one or two wrong decisions we made in the past? Yes, with hindsight it's easy to say it was a bad decision, but at the time it was probably made with the best of intentions. So forgive yourself and move on!

On the other hand, if you intentionally hurt someone else, go to them and ask for their forgiveness. Tell them how you felt at the time and ask them to try to understand. More often than not, simply reaching out will be all that's required and they'll forgive you. You can then forgive yourself and move on. If they're too petty to forgive you, the act of reaching out will make you feel better and you can justifiably forgive yourself.

In every case, recognize that whatever happened can't be changed and that, if you want a chance of a better life, it needs to be dealt with once and for all. Then look for the lessons that can be learned and see the event as an opportunity to help you do better now and in the future.

The truly wonderful thing is that there is always something good to be learned from every situation. There's always a silver lining! All we have to do is be open to looking for it. Once we get over the hurt and bitterness—once we forgive—we open ourselves to learning the lessons and growing as a person. Life's biggest and most valuable lessons come from times of difficulty (we don't learn much when things are going smoothly), so learn to appreciate this and make a habit of looking for the good in every situation.

Life takes on a whole new brightness when we are able to release the past and start focusing on the present. Not only do we experience the relief that the weight is off our shoulders, but we are now able to look forward to the future unencumbered by the past. It is truly liberating! So whatever your hang-up with the past is, deal with it, flush it, and start afresh. It's not for nothing that Jesus told us to forgive *seventy times seven!*

Write down whatever you are "unforgiving" about.

_____

_____

_____

_____

_____

_____

Write down what you can do to rectify the situation.

_____

_____

_____

_____

_____

Make a list of the lesson(s) you can learn from the situation.

_____

_____

_____

_____

_____

_____

Write a concise statement expressing your gratitude for the lesson(s) learned and how you will apply them in the future. Say something like *"I'm so happy and grateful that...."*

_____

_____

_____

_____

_____

Add this to your others and read aloud every day.

WELL DONE! YOU'VE REACHED THE END OF PART ONE.

By now, if you've worked through the exercises at the end of each chapter, you'll have compiled a rough *mission statement* for your life. This describes what your ideal life looks like and the attitudes, values, and principles you'll need to create it. Take some time now to refine and polish it.

Nothing is more important to your success than knowing exactly what it is that you want and the belief that you are worthy of, and capable of, achieving it. With what you now know, you should have no difficulty in creating the life you've always dreamed of.

I want to urge you to refer to this mission statement often, to regularly revise it, and to make it a working, living road map for your life. Read it aloud every day.

In Part Two we're going to look at some *success habits* that will ensure your continual progress toward the dream life you've designed for yourself and those close to you. This is the action part—where the rubber meets the road! Developing these success habits will ensure that your success and self-fulfillment will be a certainty and that the journey will be enjoyable.

As the slogan says, *"Just do it!"*

You can!

Part Two

SUCCESS HABITS

Chapter 23

GOALS 1

*"Goals are as essential to
success as air is to life."*
—**DAVID J. SCHWARTZ**

Goal setting—it's the one habit that every speaker I've listened to and every book I've read lists as the foundation stone of success. Having clearly defined goals focuses our minds, and what we focus on we attract into our lives.

The reason setting goals is so important is beautifully summed up in the following quote from Charles "Tremendous" Jones: *"Everyone has a success mechanism and a failure mechanism. The failure mechanism goes off by itself. The success mechanism only goes off with a goal. Every time we write down and talk about a goal we push the button to start the success mechanism."*

This is vividly illustrated by a study of graduates over a 20-year period. The study showed that the 3 percent who started out with clearly defined, written goals for their futures achieved more in financial terms than the 97 percent combined who didn't have clearly defined goals! The study also measured many other aspects of their lives—health, happiness, relationships, etc.—and the 3 percent consistently did better than the rest.

Here's a simple and effective five-step strategy that you can use to help you set goals:

1. Decide *exactly* what it is you want. You can do this for each area of your life—mental, spiritual, financial, health, relationships. The bottom line is you need to spend some time seriously thinking about exactly how you want your life to be— this year, next year, five, and ten years from now.

2. Write out a clear description of what you want. Write this in detail, specifying exactly what you want, by when, and what you intend to do to achieve it. Remember there is no such thing as something for nothing. In order to achieve our goals we must be willing to pay the price for them, generally by offering service. For example, if your goal is to have a fantastic marriage, you need to become a fantastic spouse. You will have to decide what you need to do to become this.

3. Print the key points on a card and laminate it. Carry it with you and read it daily, morning and evening. Put up pictures of the things you want or create posters stating what it is you want to achieve. Put these where you will see them most often—on your car visor, on the fridge, on the mirror, in your drawer at work. One speaker I

heard made a plaque that stood on his desk. Facing the customer it said something along the lines of, "Our aim is to please." On the side facing him it spelled out his goal—to be his own boss. *Freedom!* He read it hundreds of times each day. This may seem a little strange if you've never heard it before, but it's vital. The pictures, posters, and your laminated statement all help to keep your mind focused on your goal. As we've already learned, what we focus on we attract.

4. Now make a detailed plan of action of what you are going to do this week to move you toward the achievement of your goals. *Weekly action goals* are the stepping stones to greatness. So often we get discouraged when we have huge goals that take a long time to achieve, because we can't control the future. We can, however, control what we are going to do this week, and each step that takes us closer to our goal is encouragement and proof that we can succeed. Break your weekly action goals down into *daily action plans* and commit yourself to doing whatever it takes to carry them out.

5. At the end of each week evaluate your progress, set a new action goal for the next week, and go for it.

Following these five steps is simple but not easy. It requires some serious self-discipline, but the more you do it the easier it will become. The rewards will far exceed your expectations!

Work through the five step process for each area of your life—spiritual, physical, mental, relational, social, career, and financial.

Write a concise statement outlining your goals as if you have already achieved them. Say something like, *"I'm so happy and grateful that I am financially free, fit, healthy, etc."* This will form part of your *self-talk*.

Read aloud every day.

Chapter 24

GOALS 2

*"Although goals are important, having
a plan of action is vital to the success of
those goals. Having a goal with no plan
of action is like wanting to travel to a new
destination without having a map."*
—STEVE MARABOLI

What practical steps can we take to ensure that we achieve our goals?

If you're anything like me, you never had anyone teach you about the importance of setting goals, and planning how to achieve them, during all the years at school and college. I'm so thankful that we were introduced to a network marketing opportunity, because it was here that I was first exposed to the importance of goal setting.

So let's take a step-by-step look at what we need to do, once we've set our goals. As I mentioned in the previous chapter, Step 4 in the five-step goal setting process is breaking the goal down into a *weekly action goal* and then into a *daily action plan*. Doing this is one of the most important things I've learned about achieving my goals. When we first started out, we set huge goals but didn't break them down into manageable chunks. We didn't come close to achieving them and became discouraged. We even started thinking that setting goals didn't work!

Let's assume that the goal is to earn X amount in commissions this year and that in order to do this we need to sell $1,000 each week. If we allow that we will work five days a week, then it's pretty simple to work out that we need to sell $200 each day in order to accomplish the goal. So our *daily action plan* needs to be a detailed plan of how we're going to do this.

Before the week starts, we need to decide exactly who we are going to call on each day and how we can best help them get what they need from what we offer (our products or services). Then each day we make sure we call on those people and sell them what they need. The important thing here is that we plan our week before it starts, because doing so gives our subconscious mind time to work and come up with ideas that will help us achieve our daily targets. Many top earners plan their next week on Friday afternoon, so their subconscious has all weekend to work on the plan.

The next important step is to constantly evaluate our progress (Step 5 in the goal setting process). At the end of each day, take stock of what you have achieved and alter tomorrow's target if required. For example, if you've only sold $180 today, adjust the plan to do $220 tomorrow. Again, the key is to do this before the next day starts, so do it before you leave work or before going to bed. Once again, you're giving your subconscious mind time to work.

The important thing here is to understand that each day's results are not to be seen as success or failure, but simply a step on the way to achieving the weekly action goal. It's easier to catch up a little each day than to get to Friday and discover that you're way short of your goal with not enough time to catch up—a sure way to become discouraged.

A word of warning here—if you've exceeded your target for the day, *don't* reduce tomorrow's target! It's all too easy to relax after a good day and not push as hard tomorrow. Before you know it, you'll have relaxed a few days in a row and be way behind target.

This is a very simple example, but the principle can be applied to any goal—financial, social, physical, or mental. The key is developing the discipline of doing something daily to move us in the direction of our goals. The exciting thing here is that doing this consistently will result in it becoming a habit, and habits shape our futures.

List the five most important goals in your life right now (see the list you made in the previous chapter on goals).

_____

_____

_____

_____

_____

Now list the actions you need to take this week to move you closer to achieving these five goals. Be specific.

_____

_____

_____

_____

_____

Write a detailed plan of what you need to do each day this week to make sure you accomplish what you listed above. Review your daily action plan every evening and adjust as necessary to ensure you stay on target.

_____

_____

_____

_____

_____

Redo this exercise every week, setting new weekly action goals and making new daily action plans.

Chapter 25

ACTION

*"Achievement seems to be connected
with action. Successful men and
women keep moving. They make
mistakes, but they don't quit."*
—CONRAD HILTON

The habit of taking action is the next key to success. As a good friend says, *"Action brings success."* Without action nothing can happen. While this seems obvious, many people struggle with taking action and end up frustrated, going nowhere.

So what will help us develop the action habit?

First is knowing exactly what it is we want. Lack of clearly defined dreams, and the goals needed to achieve them, is the surest way to end up going nowhere in life. Clearly defined, written down dreams and goals simplify life enormously. Every decision we need to make becomes simple when weighed against whether it will move us in the direction of our dreams or not. When we know exactly what we want, the needless frustration and indecision disappear from our lives, and deciding on what action to take next becomes clear.

Second is understanding that failure is an event, not a life sentence. Too many people are afraid to take action in case it doesn't produce the result wanted. Doing nothing most certainly will produce nothing. Taking action, however, can only move us in the direction we want to go. It's important to understand that not every decision will be the right one, but we only have to make 51 good ones out of 100 to be succeeding. It's much easier to change course once we are moving than it is to get going, so move! If, as we learned in Chapter 22, the best, most successful managers only get it right 30 percent of the time, surely we can forgive ourselves for the occasional wrong decision. The important thing is to understand that it's by making mistakes that we learn and that a mistake isn't failure. The only time we fail is when we stop trying.

As long as we are doing something, we have a chance of succeeding. Doing nothing, on the other hand, is a guarantee of failure. As bestselling author and business coach Michael Masterton says, *"Ready, Fire, Aim!"* His point is that once we make a decision (*ready*) to act (*fire*) we can change course (*aim*) as we progress.

So get into the action habit. Setting weekly action goals is the most important thing you can do to ensure you succeed. Adjust your course as often as is needed, but keep on doing something and you'll be astounded by what you achieve.

Go back to the previous chapter on goals and relook at your weekly action goals and your daily action plans. Are they really moving you toward your dreams or just keeping you busy?

Chapter 26

VISUALIZATION

"I believe that visualization is one of the most
powerful means of achieving personal goals."
—HARVEY MACKAY

In this chapter let's focus on another success habit—visualization.

Visualization is simply imagining yourself already having done what you want to do. Top sportsmen and women do it all the time. How many of you have seen footage of Hestrie Cloete, the South African high jumper, just before she goes to jump? Her eyes are closed, her hands are turning circles around each other, mimicking her body going over the bar. She's seeing herself sailing over the bar. I'll bet she also sees herself on the winner's podium receiving the gold medal.

So why is visualization so important to success? Simply because it raises our subconscious mind's awareness of what it is we want to do. By doing this, we are opening ourselves to the full potential of our subconscious, which will attract all we require to succeed. *"Now hang on!"* I hear some of you saying. *"Do you really expect me to believe that everything it takes to succeed is already in place?"* Yes, that's exactly what I'm saying!

Think about it this way—did every great inventor really invent whatever made them famous? Did Newton invent gravity, Marconi radio waves, Edison electricity, or did they merely figure out how to work what was already there?

It's pretty obvious, isn't it? They simply figured out how to work what had been there since the beginning of creation. By focusing their minds on whatever it was that they wanted to achieve, they succeeded and today are immortalized as the greats in history. You see, by constantly seeing (focusing on) what it is you want to achieve, you will attract the required ideas, people, and resources to yourself.

Sounds almost too good to be true doesn't it? Well, it is true. As Andrew Matthews (author of one of my favorite books, *Being Happy*) puts it: *"We gravitate toward our dominant thoughts."* By constantly thinking about and picturing ourselves succeeding, we are harnessing the Law of Attraction and allowing our subconscious mind to go to work on our behalf.

Bob Proctor talks about *"being in the right place at the right time."* But, he says, it's no good being in the right place at the right time if you're not aware that you are. It's the awareness that counts, and that comes from constantly thinking about and visualizing what you want to achieve.

So no matter what it is that you want in life, never stop seeing yourself as already having succeeded. Think about it all the time, dream about it, talk about it, and sooner or later you'll find that the ideas, the people, and the resources will become available.

Follow the advice of Alfred A. Montapert: *"To accomplish great things we must first dream, then visualize, then plan... believe...act!"*

List all the things you dream of doing (go back to the chapter on dreams to refresh your memory).

_____

_____

_____

_____

_____

Now write down how you see yourself when you achieve each of your dreams. Be very specific; think about how you'll feel, what you'll think, who'll be there to celebrate with you, etc.

_____

_____

_____

If you haven't already created a goals poster (see Chapter 23), write your dreams on a large piece of card and add pictures and slogans of what you intend to do. Put this dream chart somewhere where you'll see it every day. Use it to help you keep your goals and dreams vivid and clear in your mind.

Chapter 27

PERSISTENCE 1

"Nothing in the world can take the place of persistence. Talent will not; nothing is more common than an unsuccessful man with talent. Genius will not; unrewarded genius is almost a proverb. Education will not; the world is full of educated derelicts. Persistence and determination alone are omnipotent. The slogan 'Press on' has solved, and always will solve, the problems of the human race."
—CALVIN COOLIDGE

Some time back I read an interesting article by Craig Ballantyne in which he talks about lessons we can learn from the movie *The Shawshank Redemption*. It's about one man's struggle to survive in prison and how he finally triumphs over injustice (he is innocent) and adversity. The main lesson is about persistence—keeping on keeping on, never giving up. As Mr. Ballantyne puts it, *"chipping away until you succeed."*

This is probably one of the biggest secrets to success, and there are countless stories of people who quit just before success came. But rather than focus on the quitters, let's take a look at some of those men and women who didn't quit and, as a result, succeeded beyond their wildest dreams. (By the way, to succeed beyond your wildest dreams you have to have some wild dreams to start with!)

Let's start with someone really well known, like Thomas Edison. He's reported to have tried approximately 10,000 times before he perfected the incandescent light bulb.

Now that's chipping away! When asked how it felt to have failed so many times he replied, *"We didn't fail, we just found ten thousand ways it didn't work."* A real winning attitude, I think.

Or how about Jack Canfield and Mark Victor Hansen, authors of the Chicken Soup books. They took their first book, *Chicken Soup for the Soul,* to over 100 publishers before they found one willing to publish it. Once it was published, they struggled for two years to get it sold. But the rest is history—it became a publishing legend, broke all kinds of records, earned a place in the Guinness Book of Records, and made both of them multi-millionaires.

These are wonderful examples of chipping away and not giving up, not expecting instant gratification. The world is full of success stories like these. Persistence is vital for success whether in business, sport, entertainment, or relationships.

So what is it that keeps people keeping on, in spite of all the challenges? Simply this: clearly defined dreams and goals and the determination to keep on chipping away until they succeed. You'll never know what you're capable of until you try, and you'll never know the sweet taste of success unless you never stop trying.

This week take time to remember all the times you succeeded because you refused to quit.

Think in terms of relationships, sports, academic achievements, employment, or any other occasion.

_____

_____

_____

_____

_____

Write a short statement summarizing your success. For example: *"I succeed because I persist...."*

_____

_____

_____

_____

_____

_____

_____

Add it to your others and read aloud every day.

Chapter 28

PERSISTENCE 2

"We first make our habits, then
our habits make us."
—JOHN DRYDEN

In the previous chapter, we learned that persistence is one of the hallmarks of winners. I was thinking about this recently and it struck me that persistence could also be described as one of the hallmarks of losers!

You're probably thinking that I'm a bit off track here, but consider this: losers make a habit of doing things that prevent them from succeeding. They persist with their bad habits! Actually, when you think about it, it's mostly habits that make the difference between success and failure. Winners make a habit of doing what losers are unwilling to do.

So let's take a look at a few losing habits that most of us have and that we need to overcome if we are to achieve our dreams.

The first, and probably the most common, is *procrastination*. It truly is the thief of time, and because time is not hours and minutes but a portion of our life, it's a thief of our lives! Procrastination is most common when we have no goals, nothing to give us direction. Having clearly defined goals helps us make decisions, because we can weigh every choice we need to make against whether it is going to move us toward or away from our goals. So if procrastination is chipping away at your life, check on your goals and decide to adopt an attitude of *do it now.*

Lack of self-discipline is another habit that separates winners from losers. Being punctual, courteous, conscientious, and organized are winning traits and will attract people to us. The opposites, while making for a seemingly easier life, will alienate people. I think self-discipline stems from our core values. It takes time and effort to think about what's important to us, but once we have clearly defined our core values they help us to lead more disciplined and ultimately more successful lives.

Not taking responsibility for our actions will also play havoc with our success. Constantly blaming circumstances, or others, for our lack of success is one of the quickest ways to ensure failure. Everything we do is a result of choices we make, and, while we can allow others to influence us, at the end of the day it's our call and no one else's.

Failing to plan is another losing habit. Flying by the seat of your pants may seem like a cool way to live, but in reality winners make a point of planning everything in advance. As the saying goes, *"Proper preparation prevents poor performance."* So whatever you're about to do, prior planning will always ensure a better result. Coupled with planning is analysis—thinking about what we have done and figuring out if we could have done it better. Really successful people try to plan for every eventuality before they embark on a course of action and spend time reviewing their performance so they can do better next time.

This week take a look at your weak areas and decide on a course of action to change them from weaknesses to strengths.

List your stumbling blocks below, and alongside each one list the stepping stone you are going to turn it into.

STUMBLING BLOCK	STEPPING STONE

STUMBLING BLOCK	STEPPING STONE

Now summarize your new stepping stones into a statement. Say something like, *"I am excellent at...."*

_____

_____

_____

_____

_____

_____

_____

_____

_____

_____

Add it to your previous statements and read aloud every day.

Chapter 29

SELF-TALK

"Guess who's the number one person
you communicate with on a daily basis?
It's you! Our internal conversations
characterize how we view the world
and influence every part of our lives—
relationships, achievements, attitude and
ultimately our degree of happiness."
—TODD SMITH

One of the most common things that holds people back in life is a poor self-image. It's not all that surprising when one considers all the negative input we get growing up. According to Murray Smith and John Assaraf, authors of *The Answer*, by the time we reach 17 we've had an average of 150,000 negatives (*"No you can't,"* etc.) and only 5,000 positives (*"Yes you can"*). That's 30 nos for every yes! Is it any wonder that most people end up with a less than perfect self-image?

The truth is that there is nothing you cannot do (physical limitations aside) if you believe you can and are determined. So what holds us back? As I've already stated, we are our own worst enemies because we constantly tell ourselves negative things. So let's take a good look at *self-talk*. Remembering that the majority of our conversations are with ourselves, what we say to ourselves is crucial to our self-image.

The key is understanding and accepting that only we can decide how we think, and that what we think about most becomes our reality. What we say to ourselves repeatedly has a huge impact on how we think and thus on our success or failure. Controlling our self-talk is therefore vitally important.

If we're continuously putting ourselves down, downplaying our abilities, we can never succeed. This is because the subconscious mind will only allow us to achieve what's consistent with our self-image. If, for instance, we have a mental picture of ourselves as a fat person, it will be very hard to lose weight. Why?—because our subconscious will keep us doing whatever will maintain the picture it has of us—in this instance, being fat. We have to first change the picture we have of ourselves in our subconscious mind before we can change.

The interesting thing about the subconscious is that it doesn't reason. It will accept whatever we put into it as fact. Think of it as the hard drive in your computer. It simply stores information and regurgitates it on request. In computer terms there's a saying: *"Garbage in—garbage out."* The same applies to our subconscious. What we tell ourselves repeatedly has a very powerful impact on our subconscious mind. I once heard someone describe it as being like scratching a piece of wood with a sharp nail. One scratch will make a small mark on the wood. Repeated scratches will make a deep groove.

This is why our self-talk is so important. If it's constantly negative, it's creating "deep negative grooves" in our subconscious. The only way to overcome this is to change what we say to ourselves—to start creating "deep positive grooves." This is the starting place for changing our self-image. The best way to start is to write out a formal self-talk listing all the things we want in our lives. The subconscious doesn't recognize the difference between *"I'm debt free"* and *"I'm in debt."* It focuses on *debt*, so rather say, *"I'm financially free."* Similarly, it's no good saying *"I'm going to be..."*—we need to say *"I am..."* for it to make a positive impression on the subconscious.

The bottom line is to start talking what we do want but don't have yet, instead of constantly talking about what we do have but don't want! The more passion and enthusiasm we use when doing this, the more impact it has. The more often we read our self-talk, the quicker it will penetrate the subconscious, so read it aloud many times a day. Once there, the subconscious accepts it as fact and starts looking for information to support it. It starts to supply us with information that enables what we are saying to become reality.

The first step is to determine exactly what we want. We've already done this in previous chapters, writing down exactly what we want in all areas of our lives. Make sure you've been specific, as the mind cannot focus on generalities. For instance, it's no good saying, *"I want more money."* Five dollars is more. So determine exactly how much you want.

Once you've sorted out all your wants, draft them into a statement of fact, as if you already have them. The subconscious can't act on something that might happen, so instead of saying *"I'm going to have"* say *"I have"* (even if you don't have it yet). The subconscious doesn't know the difference between fact and fiction, it simply accepts whatever we feed it!

It's important to write and say everything in positive terms, in the present tense and with emotion and excitement. The more emotion involved, the more impact it has on our subconscious. Keep the sentences short and sharp, easy to say and remember. Bob Proctor suggests that we say: *"I'm so happy and grateful that...."*

Once you've decided exactly what you want in your self-talk, it's a good idea to print it on a small card, laminate it, and keep it in your pocket or bag. Read it aloud as many times a day as possible, with emotion and meaning. Do it first thing in the morning, as you're driving to work, during the day, and especially last thing at night before going to sleep. Your subconscious will then have all night to work on it. By the same token, the very worst thing you can do is watch the late night news. You're giving your subconscious all that negativity to dwell on all night. Is it any wonder people wake up feeling depressed?

Now if you're seeing this for the first time and find it a bit much to accept, as I did, consider the following. Have you ever struggled with a problem that you couldn't solve and woken up in the middle of the night with the solution clear in your mind? Probably all of us have experienced this at some time in our lives. That's the subconscious mind working. Because you were focused on the problem, your subconscious went to work and came up with the solution.

The same process will apply when you want to change something in your life. You just have to supply the focus! Gino Norris has this to say about self-talk: *"Your self-talk is the channel of behavior change."*

Here are some ideas you can use:

- I'm so happy and grateful that my marriage is fantastic and that my spouse is the best partner I could ever wish for!

- I'm so happy and grateful that my kids are excelling at school; they're responsible, considerate, and a joy to be with!

- I'm so happy and grateful that my job is stimulating and fulfilling and I get regular promotions!

- I'm so happy and grateful that I earn $_____ and have more than enough to meet all my needs and to help others!

Saying things like this to yourself many times each day is important if you want to change your life. Keep on changing your self-talk as things change in your life. For instance, when you achieve a goal, rewrite your self-talk to include your new goals.

What you say is what you get!

Think about the things you say to yourself often every day. Are they positive or negative? Write them down.

_____

_____

_____

_____

_____

Now rewrite them so that they are all positive. For example, if you often think, *"I don't feel well,"* change it to, *"I'm so happy and grateful that I'm fit and healthy."*

_____

_____

_____

_____

Print them on a card and read aloud, many times every day.

Chapter 30

SELF-EDUCATION

"Formal education will make you a living;
self-education will make you a fortune."
—JIM ROHN

In today's fast-changing world we need to be constantly learning new skills and re-inventing ourselves in order to succeed (and keep succeeding). Continuous learning is what is going to separate the successful from the average.

Never before in history has change been as fast and as dramatic. Think about it—our great-grandparents, and even some of our grandparents, lived lives that were pretty much the same from birth to death. They knew exactly what was going on around them because it was the same as what happened to their parents and grandparents. Today, things change daily. It's still incredible to me that only sixty-odd years after the Wright brothers first flew, a man walked on the moon.

The phrase *change and succeed* has never been more relevant than it is today. Eric Hoffer, author and philosopher, made a remarkable statement some years ago. He said: *"In times of change the learners will inherit the earth, while the learned will find themselves beautifully equipped to handle a world that no longer exists."* It's worth reading this a few times and letting it sink in.

Bob Proctor says that there is no such thing as an educated individual. There are only those who are learning and those who are not. Those who think that learning stopped when school stopped will soon find themselves severely disadvantaged in the marketplace. There are many people who have wonderful academic qualifications but who are failing financially. At the same time, there are many out there with a very basic education who are making fortunes. The obvious conclusion is that formal education isn't a prerequisite for success.

So what is?

One study of engineers noted that their success in the market place was only 15 percent due to their engineering skills and 85 percent due to their people skills. Isn't it strange that we were taught little or nothing about people skills throughout our school and university years!

Another famous study I've already mentioned tracked a graduating class from one of the finest universities in the US. After twenty years, those graduates who had started out with clearly defined, written goals for the future had achieved more in financial terms than all those who did not have written goals. The really interesting part is that only 3 percent of the graduating class had written goals to start with! They achieved more, financially speaking, than the 97 percent combined who did not! Again, isn't it strange that we were taught very little about goal setting at school or university?

These are just two examples of things we need to learn that are vital for our success, but which we need to teach ourselves. There are obviously many more things we need to learn to keep pace with the changes taking place around us. The point is, it's up to us to educate ourselves. The exciting thing is that there has never been more information available to us than there is today.

We need to decide what it is that we want to achieve in life, then go and equip ourselves with the knowledge and skills required to do so. Those who do will surely *"inherit the earth!"*!

This week take some time to think about what you are doing to improve your knowledge and skills. Think in terms of your relationships, career, social life, and spiritual life. If you're not doing anything on an ongoing basis, write down below what you intend to do to rectify the situation.

- Relationships

_____

_____

_____

• Career

• Social life

• Spiritual life

Write a concise statement saying what you are going to do to increase your knowledge and skills. Remembering what we learned about self-talk, it needs to be in the present tense— *"I'm always learning new ways to...."*

_____

_____

_____

_____

_____

_____

_____

Add it to your other statements and read aloud every day.

Chapter 31

READING

*"No matter how busy you may think you
are, you must find time for reading, or
surrender yourself to self-chosen ignorance."*
—CONFUCIUS

Let's look at another important success habit—reading.

Can reading really be critical to our success? Yes, it is a habit endorsed by every success book, speaker, CD, and DVD I've read, listened to, or watched.

There's a wonderful quote from Abraham Lincoln that sums it up beautifully: *"A capacity, and taste, for reading gives access to whatever has already been discovered by others."* The bottom line is that everything we need to know to succeed has already been written down by someone. All we have to do is read it!

We were all taught that *experience is the best teacher.* It's not true! Like so many things we were taught, it's a half truth. The truth is, *other people's experience is the best teacher.* You see, for any one of us to experience everything we need to know about success, we'd have to have lived right from the start of creation! But by reading, we can pick up all that wisdom in a relatively short space of time.

Now, it's obvious that what we read is important. Newspapers and most popular magazines are not going to contribute to our success. Neither are romances, westerns, thrillers, and other works of popular fiction. We need to read books that can inspire, educate, and equip us to succeed in our fields of endeavor. Biographies of successful people, motivation and self-improvement books, and how-to books are all worth their weight in gold.

Here are some classic self-help books (see the Recommended Reading list at the end of the book for more):

- *How to Win Friends and Influence People* by Dale Carnegie
- *Think and Grow Rich* by Napoleon Hill
- *The Magic of Thinking Big and its successor, The Magic of Thinking Success,* by David Schwartz
- *The Greatest Salesman in the World* by Og Mandino
- My personal favorite, *Being Happy* by Andrew Matthews

Each of these has the power to positively change your life forever! Excitingly, you can probably find all of them in secondhand book shops for very little. I even found *Think and Grow Rich* as a free download on the Internet! Sadly, many people buy them and never really study them, missing out on the priceless wisdom they contain.

What if you're not a good reader?

Brian Tracy offers this advice:

> *"If you are not a good reader, make the decision, right now, that you are going to go any distance, pay any price, overcome any obstacle, and spend whatever amount of money it takes to become an excellent reader. If you do not know how to read particularly well, stop everything else that you are doing outside of your work and dedicate yourself to reading. Spend every spare minute reading as if your future depends on it. **Because it does.** It may take a week, a month, or a year to become a better reader. It may take even longer. But that doesn't matter. Becoming an excellent reader will kick open doors of opportunity that you cannot now imagine."*

The emphasis on the words "*because it does*" is mine—I believe it's that important! So start today. Be sure to read something every day that can help you move toward your dreams and goals. Even if all you do is read something positive for just 15 minutes every night before you go to sleep, the benefits will be worth the effort.

Leaders are readers.

Make a list of the books you have read in the last month (or a few months). Next to each make a note—yes or no—if the book increased your knowledge about any topic that will help you move forward in life.

_____

_____

_____

_____

_____

Now make a list of books you intend to read in the next months that will help you move toward your dreams and goals (use the Recommended Reading list at the end of the book as a starting place).

_____

_____

_____

_____

_____

Write a short sentence saying what you have decided to do in order to feed your mind by reading every day. Say something like, *"I read a positive book for at least 15 minutes every day."*

_____

_____

_____

_____

_____

Add it to your previous ones and read aloud every day.

Chapter 32

COMMUNICATION 1

*"The way we communicate with
others and with ourselves ultimately
determines the quality of our lives."*
—ANTHONY ROBBINS

On the face of it, communication doesn't sound like something that's vital to our success, yet studies show that no single factor better predicts your future income than the size of your vocabulary! That really made me stop and think—how about you?

Communication is rapidly becoming a lost art. We no longer talk to each other—we text, e-mail, Facebook, and tweet. Grammar and spelling have gone out the window and abbreviations are a whole new language, along with emoticons. But can a smiley face ☺ ever convey as much as:

*"Loved you yesterday, love you still,
Always have, always will."*

There's so much more to a conversation than just the words spoken. What about the tone, the expressions, hand movements, body language, smiles—all of which can never be replicated in text. There's also the sharing of minds, of one idea leading to another and the sum being so much greater than the parts. There's a magic in sharing with friends, be it joyful or sorrowful, that can never be matched by a quick text or e-mail.

Studies of prisoners serving time in jail have revealed a definite correlation between vocabulary and violence. The smaller the vocabulary, the greater the tendency to violent behavior—it's as if the violence stems from the inability to express what's important to that individual. Then there's the opposite side of the coin—those who speak well generally get the job, the contract, the sale, the girl/boy. A good vocabulary and the ability to speak well also help raise one's self-image and self-confidence.

As important as speaking well is writing well. The ability to put ideas and information down on paper in a concise, clear way is important to our success. This is possibly more crucial today than ever before, given that we routinely work and trade on a global scale. Can you imagine what would happen if a contract for a multi-million deal was worded in such a way that there could be confusion as to what was being agreed upon? Multi-million lawsuits!

History teaches us that many of the world's greatest leaders were also the greatest communicators. It's just that much easier to get someone to follow you if you can inspire and motivate them, and that requires eloquence. Winston Churchill was a master of the English language, whether spoken or written. In fact, his writings financed his life for most of his career. (In those days, politicians didn't earn the millions they do today; they were still public *servants*!) He had a wonderful way with words and a lightning fast wit. On one occasion Lady Astor said to him, *"If you were my husband, I'd give you poison."*

He instantly replied, *"Madam, if I were your husband, I'd take it!"* Oh, to be able to come up with a reply like that when it's needed!

Some time back the movie *The King's Speech* was on circuit. It portrayed the courage and immense effort that King George VI of England displayed in overcoming his severe stutter. By doing so, he was able to make speeches that inspired and encouraged the English people at a time when they were enduring tremendous hardships during World War II.

So make it a goal to learn a new word every day, to improve your spelling and grammar, and to become a better communicator. Doing so will improve your self-confidence, your finances, and make your whole life better.

Make a list of all the things you intend to do to improve your communication skills.

_____

_____

_____

Summarize them into a concise statement.

_____

_____

_____

_____

Add it to your others and read aloud every day.

Chapter 33

COMMUNICATION 2

*"Communication is a skill that you can learn.
It's like riding a bicycle or typing. If you're
willing to work at it, you can rapidly improve
the quality of every part of your life."*
—BRIAN TRACY

To continue the subject of communication, it's worth knowing that fully 85 percent of your success will be due to your ability to communicate effectively. This even applies to professions like computer programming, engineering, and accounting. To succeed in any profession (and especially parenting—the most important of all professions!), one needs to be able to communicate well.

So what makes for good communication? Albert Mehrabian, Professor Emeritus at UCLA, proposed that in any conversation, our words only account for 7 percent of the impact on those listening. Our tone of voice and our body language account for 93 percent—38 percent and 55 percent respectively! If we accept this as being true, then we realize that communication is much more than just saying the right words. People are intuitive beings, and our subconscious mind picks up on signals from all our senses, not just our hearing.

Here are some tips from experts like Brian Tracy and others that will help us become better communicators.

First, look at and lean toward the person you're speaking to. Ever had the situation where you're speaking to someone and they're looking out of the window, at their feet, or anywhere else except you? Didn't it make you feel that they weren't really interested or not taking you seriously? Pay close attention to the person you're talking to—your subconscious mind will pick up all kinds of clues. More importantly, they'll feel like you're really interested in what they have to say. Next, get down to their level, especially when you're talking to children. No one likes someone towering over them, so getting to the same level as the other person makes them more comfortable and thus more likely to listen.

I have a mentor who, when he speaks with you, makes you feel that you are the most important person in the world at that moment. He looks intently at you all the time and never interrupts. People who meet him come away impressed and often comment what a great person he is. He is a great person, and his communication skills make this immediately apparent to people, so they're more likely to listen to him.

Second, seek first to understand, then to be understood. Too often we are so busy trying to get our point of view across that we don't stop to hear what the other person has to say. Giving the other person a chance to state their case and making sure we understand exactly where they're coming from makes them much more likely to listen to us.

Third, pause before replying. This gives you time to think about your reply, but more importantly it gives your listener the impression that you're taking what they said seriously. Again, this will make them more open to hearing what you have to say.

Fourth, ask clarifying questions. This ties in with the second point and is vital to making sure that you're both on the same wavelength. Questions like *"Did you mean...?"* or *"Could you go through that again?"* not only help you understand exactly what they mean, but also make them feel you really care about what they are saying.

Last, paraphrase what they have said back to them. Saying something like *"As I understand you..."* or *"So you mean that..."* shows the other person that you are listening and that you have understood what they are saying. Again, this will make them more sympathetic to what you're going to say.

Communication can make or break our chances of success in our careers, in business, and in our relationships. It's worth taking the time and effort to develop into a skillful communicator.

Learn to communicate well and prosper!

Revise last week's exercises using what you've learned this week.

Chapter 34

COMMUNICATION 3

*"Confusion grows in direct proportion
to the number of words used."*
—**NIDO QUBEIN**

In the previous two chapters we looked at how important communication is to our success. Recently, I read an article on the subject by Nido Qubein, an international speaker and accomplished author on sales, communication, and leadership. In the article, Qubein lists six techniques that we can use to increase our effectiveness as verbal communicators, which I think are worth learning and applying.

They are:

1. *Think before You Speak*

Mr. Qubein states that the most common sources of confusion are:

- Not clearly thinking through what it is we want to get across, resulting in a muddled message.

- Having so much to say that we can't possibly say it all.

- Having such a strong opinion that we can't keep it in.

Our objective should always be to convey as simply and clearly as possible exactly what it is we want to get across to our listener. We can only do this if we take the time to clearly think through what it is we want to say, organizing our thoughts and putting our brain into gear before we open our mouth. The benefits will be multiple. Not only will we avoid misunderstandings, but by taking time to think about what we are about to say we'll often avoid putting our foot in it!

2. *Saying What We Mean and Only What We Mean*

Too often misunderstandings come because we say things we don't really mean. We embroider, exaggerate, or bend the truth just a little and then, in order not to seem to have lied, we are forced to lie. If we stick to the truth every time, we'll never have to resort to trying to save face.

3. *Get to the Point*

Again, many misunderstandings result from beating about the bush and not saying exactly what we want to say. If you want someone to do something, ask them to do it in plain and simple language. Can't be simpler than that!

4. *Less Is More—Be Concise and to the Point*

Avoid long complicated explanations and complicated words. Keep it simple so there can be no misunderstanding. A good technique is to ask your listener to repeat what it was you just told them. If they can do so accurately, you know you did a good job of communicating.

5. *Be Yourself—Don't Try to Be Who or What You Are Not*

People are quick to sense a fake. We all have our own unique personalities, our own way of expressing ourselves. Be natural. You'll be more comfortable, and therefore more convincing.

6. *Paint Word Pictures*

As the saying goes, "a picture is worth a thousand words." People think in images. For example, if I mention a dog, you don't spell D-O-G in your mind, you see a picture of a dog. Therefore, if we use words that help people visualize what we want them to understand, we make our words that much more effective.

Learning and consciously applying these six points will have a profound effect on our effectiveness as communicators. Verbal communication is our most frequent way of communicating, and so it is really important.

Remember, however, that speaking is only one half of communicating. We have to listen as well. The most successful communicators (who generally just happen to be the most successful people, have the best relationships, earn the most money, etc.) are those individuals who listen well. In fact, often saying very little but listening intently will bring results far in excess of anything you can say!

Write down the steps you're going to take to improve your verbal communication skills. Think in terms of the words you use, your tone and emphasis, body language, hand motions, etc. Ask someone you think is a great speaker to help you. Consider joining an organization like Toast Masters or signing up for a public speaking course.

_____

_____

_____

_____

_____

_____

Now write a concise statement saying why you are a great speaker. Say something like, *"I'm a fantastic speaker because...."*

_____

_____

_____

_____

_____

_____

Add it to your others and read aloud every day.

Chapter 35

PEOPLE SKILLS

*"I've learned that people will forget
what you said, people will forget
what you did, but people will never
forget how you made them feel."*
—**MAYA ANGELOU**

The person who learns to get on with others will always be more successful than the one who doesn't. People skills count! One interesting study looked at engineers to ascertain why some were successful and others not. The conclusion of the researchers was that success was 85 percent due to the individual's people skills and only 15 percent due to their technical skills. We probably all know a "genius" who hasn't a clue about relating to others, possesses no people skills, and is a social misfit.

Unfortunately, people skills aren't taught in schools and universities. They ought to be! In every area of life, be it personal, business, sport, or politics, the people who end up making a lasting success are those who understand that no one can do it on their own. We all need people to help us succeed (the term "a self-made man" is a misnomer), and the relationships we build are the key.

So what can we do to improve our people skills and build good relationships? First, and most importantly, we need to have a good relationship with the most important person in our life—ourselves! The Bible teaches us that we need to love others as we love ourselves. Without a good self-image and a healthy appreciation of our own worth, we can never build secure, lasting relationships with others.

Next, we need to understand that in order to build good relationships, we have to become the kind of person with whom others want to have a relationship. In other words, we have to develop an attractive personality. The best way to do this is to become genuinely interested in others. We need to take the focus off ourselves and refocus on others. To paraphrase JFK, *"Ask not what your friends can do for you, but what you can do for them."*

Become a good listener. As the saying goes, *"God made us with two ears and one mouth!"* and as the child said to the father, *"Listen to me with your eyes, Daddy."* Many of us are so busy thinking of what we want to say next that we don't pay attention to what the other person is saying. Genuinely listening to others makes them feel important.

Become someone others can rely on. Make sure your word is your bond. When people know that what you say is what you do, every time, they will be much more likely to want to be associated with you.

Always be positive and cheerful. When people ask how you are, are they sorry they asked? Become the kind of person people are comfortable around. As someone put it, be an *"old shoe kind of person.*" Work on developing a pleasing personality, always friendly and upbeat. Refuse to gossip.

Are you a peacemaker, or are you a trouble stirrer? We've all heard the biblical phrase *"Blessed are the peacemakers"* (Matthew 5:9). If we're always adding fuel to the fire, we are not going to be the kind of person others will want to have a relationship with. On the other hand, if we develop a reputation of being someone who always looks to smooth things and broker good relationships, we will be certain to build good relationships.

In all situations ask yourself how you would like others to treat you, then take the initiative and treat them like that. You'll find people will respond in kind.

Today we are constantly advised to network. Unless we are genuinely seeking to build win-win relationships with others, all our networking will amount to very little. It could even work against us if others get the impression that we are only there to further our own interests. Relationships need to give a two-way benefit to have any chance of succeeding long term. They require constant work, and the most rewarding are those that have been built over time.

As George Eliot said, *"It's easy to say how much we love new friends, and what we think of them, but words can never trace out all the fibers that knit us to the old."*

Become a people magnet.

This week think about your people skills. Ask yourself these questions:

- Am I a good listener? _____

- A good partner? _____

- A good team player? _____

- An encourager? _____

- Do I focus on what will make others happy or am I focused on myself? _____

- Any other you think important: _____

Now write a detailed plan of what you intend to do to improve your people skills.

_____

_____

_____

_____

_____

Summarize your plan into a concise statement.

_____

_____

_____

_____

_____

Add it to your previous statements and read aloud every day.

Chapter 36

TIME MANAGEMENT

*"Lost wealth may be replaced by industry, lost
knowledge by study, lost health by temperance
or medicine, but lost time is gone forever."*
—SAMUEL SMILES

One of the characteristics of successful people is how they manage their time. Time management can truly be said to be one of the secrets of the rich. The interesting thing is that no one can actually manage time—all we can manage is our use of time.

When we stop to consider that time is not hours, minutes, and seconds (that's just how we measure time) but our life, time management becomes significant. You see, when we waste an hour we waste a piece of our life! Now when we're young, we may think that we've got all the time in the world, but in reality life is very short. So making the most productive use of the time we have makes enormous sense. As Henry Ford is quoted as saying, *"It has been my observation that most people get ahead during the time that others waste."*

I'd like to suggest that we stop thinking, and talking, in terms of time management and instead start calling it *"life management."* That's really what it is—managing our lives in the time allocated to us.

As with all things that require discipline, we need a reason to do so, which takes us back to our Dreams and Goals. If we have nothing that we're striving towards, we will have little incentive to put in the effort required to develop the discipline. Once we've got a reason, learning to manage ourselves is actually quite simple.

Here are five things we can do to improve our use of time:

1.   The first thing is to actually record what you do with your time every day. Start by jotting down every 30 minutes what you have just done. Do this for just one week. Use the table below to help you.

Now take a good hard look at what you spent most of your time doing and ask yourself *"Is this helping me move toward achieving my dreams and goals, or not?"* This exercise will more than likely astound you, and not positively! Doing this will probably be all the incentive you need to start doing something constructive to make better use of your time.

2.   The next thing is to make a list of everything you need to do tomorrow—today! All successful people do! It's called a *daily action list.* The very worst thing you can do is trust your memory. The key is to make the list today, for tomorrow. Don't wait until the morning; do it before you leave work or go to bed. Just the simple act of writing things down can, according to the experts, increase your efficiency by great percentages! Use the table below to help you.

3. Now rank the list in terms of importance. You can use any system that suits you—highlighting, numbering, whatever. A simple A-B-C method works well. Mark the most important things with an A, the less important with a B, and the least important with a C.

4. Start each day by doing the A items on your list. *Do not* start any B items until you've completed all the A items. Concentrate on completing one task at a time. Forget about multitasking—focusing on one thing at a time will increase your efficiency and decrease the time you take to complete it.

Tick off each task as you complete it. This is important—it gives you a sense of achievement and satisfaction, reinforcing the will to make the list in the first place. Once you've completed all the A items on your list, proceed to the B items. Complete them, then move on to the C items. Whatever you don't finish, carry forward to tomorrow's list. It will hopefully only be C items, which weren't very important anyway.

5. In addition to your *daily action list,* use a diary to record things in the future. A diary is an indispensable tool for anyone serious about simplifying their lives and becoming more organized. Record everything you need to do in the future as you become aware of it. Use it to schedule appointments, tasks, and time off. Refer to it every day while drawing up your daily action list for tomorrow.

The benefits of time management (or rather life management) are that it simplifies our lives, cuts the stress, and ultimately frees us up to do the things we love doing the most.

Time management is life management.

Use the following table to record your activities for the day. Repeat for the next seven days.

DATE	TIME	ACTIVITY
	7:00	
	7:30	
	8:00	
	8:30	
	9:00	
	9:30	
	10:00	
	10:30	
	11:00	
	11:30	
	12:00	
	12:30	

DATE	TIME	ACTIVITY
	1:00	
	1:30	
	2:00	
	2:30	
	3:00	
	3:30	
	4:00	
	4:30	
	5:00	
	5:30	
	6:00	
	6:30	
	7:00	
	7:30	
	8:00	
	8:30	

Use the following table to draw up your daily action list.

DATE	ACTIVITY	PRIORITY

CONGRATULATIONS, YOU'VE COMPLETED PART TWO!

Thank you for buying this book and reading it this far. By applying the knowledge you now have, you are starting out on a journey that will lead to success and happiness. By continuing to practice the *success habits,* you'll find that your life will change dramatically. You'll become a better person and have increased self-confidence and relational skills. Your effectiveness in the workplace will improve, leading to more satisfaction and increased chances of promotion. If you have your own business, you'll be better able to thrive in the marketplace and take your business to new levels.

The key is to never stop learning and growing, so keep referring to your *mission statement* and your *self-talk.* Make sure they accurately reflect how you want your life to be now and where you want to go in the future. Keep setting your *weekly action goals* and working your *daily action plans*—they really are essential to your success.

Invest in the books mentioned in the Recommended Reading section, subscribe to newsletters from some of the people mentioned in the Resource section, go to seminars, listen to self-help CDs, etc. In other words, keep on growing. One of the greatest feelings of satisfaction we can experience is the knowledge that we are making a difference. Your continued personal growth will ensure that the difference will be meaningful and beneficial.

One of the best pieces of advice I've ever been given is this: the best way to truly understand and benefit from any knowledge is to share it with someone else. Explaining and/or teaching helps to clarify our understanding and improves our ability to implement it ourselves. Besides, what you hand out comes back multiplied many times over. By sharing this knowledge with those around you, you'll be helping to change their consciousness, leading to a better life for us all.

Recommended Reading

These are just a few of the fantastic books out there that can help you change your life. Once you've studied these, never stop reading—your future depends on it!

- *Acres of Diamonds* by Russell Conwell

- *An Enemy Called Average* by John Mason

- *As a Man Thinketh* by James Allen

- *Be a People Person* by John Maxwell

- *Be the Best You Can Be* by Peter Haddon

- *Being Happy* by Andrew Matthews

- *Freedom from Fear* by Mark Matteson

- *How to Win Friends and Influence People* by Dale Carnegie

- *Let Go of What Makes You Stop* by John Mason

- *Life Is Tremendous* by Charlie "Tremendous" Jones

- *Over the Top* by Zig Ziglar

- *Rich Dad, Poor Dad* by Robert Kiyosaki

- *Skill with People* by Les Giblin

- *Success Habits* by Jack Canfield

- *The Five Major Pieces to the Life Puzzle* by Jim Rohn

- *The Fred Factor* by Mark Sanborn

- *The Greatest Salesman* by Og Mandino

- *The Magic of Thinking Big* by David Schwartz

- *The Magic of Thinking Success* by David Schwartz

- *The Seasons of Life* by Jim Rohn

- *The Seven Habits of Highly Effective People* by Stephen Covey

- *Think and Grow Rich* by Napoleon Hill

- *What You Say Is What You Get* by Don Gossett

- *Winning without Intimidation* by Bob Burg

- *You Were Born Rich* by Bob Proctor

Resources

Here are a few websites that you can check out, perhaps subscribe to their newsletters, or just download the free goodies they offer. Each one has the power to change your life. *Enjoy!*

- Alexander Green, www.spiritualwealth.com
- Andrew Matthews, www.andrewmatthews.com
- Anthony Robbins, www.anthonyrobbins.com
- Bob Proctor, www.bobproctor.com
- Brian Tracy, www.briantracy.com
- Jack Canfield, www.jackcanfield.com
- Jim Rohn, www.jimrohn.com
- Les Brown, www.lesbrown.com
- Nido Qubein, www.nidoqubein.com
- Robin Sharma, www.robinsharma.com
- *Success* Magazine, www.success.com

- TED, www.ted.com

- *The Secret*, www.thesecret.tv

- Zig Ziglar, www.zigziglar.com

These are just a few of the many great sites out there—the ones that inspire me and that I use regularly. I'd love to hear about yours. I'd also appreciate your thoughts on the book.

Please post comments on www.facebook.com/realsuccessbook.

This book is also available as an e-book from Amazon, Barnes & Noble, Flipkart, iBooks, and Smashwords.

To get a free, printable copy of the exercises and the Time Management tables go to www.realwealth.co.za/books and use the code RS2-2013EX.

ABOUT PATRICK
MATHER-PIKE

As a successful network marketing entrepreneur, Patrick Mather-Pike has helped individuals in many countries around the world to achieve success. What makes some people successful and others not, even though they may be doing the same work, has always fascinated him and prompted a closer look into what makes success. Over the last 25 years he has studied, practiced, and taught the success principles in this book. His mission is to help people, irrespective of their backgrounds, to achieve their full potential in every area of their lives.

"I'm privileged to have been exposed to exceptional individuals and their material and have read so many great books. I wanted to share the insights I've gained with people who are starting out where I was all those years ago. I believe the simplicity of the book will be helpful in giving people a basic overview of what it takes to live a successful life and inspire them to continue this life-long, exciting journey of personal development. I hope this book points them in the right direction!"

He is married to Carol and lives in Port Elizabeth, South Africa. Besides a life-long interest in personal development, he loves travelling, wide-open spaces, photography, and has a keen interest in natural health.